8710 40

W9-BCL-736

Lineberger Memorial Library

Lutheran Theological Southern Seminary   Columbia, S. C.

8710 40

Flannery O'Connor

IMAGES
OF
GRACE

by HAROLD FICKETT & DOUGLAS R. GILBERT

WILLIAM B. EERDMANS PUBLISHING COMPANY   GRAND RAPIDS, MICHIGAN

To our former
students at
Wheaton College

Copyright © 1986 by Wm. B. Eerdmans Publishing Co.
255 Jefferson Ave. S.E., Grand Rapids, MI 49503

All rights reserved
Printed in the United States of America

Library of Congress Cataloging-in-Publication Data

Fickett, Harold.
   Flannery O'Connor: images of grace.

   1. O'Connor, Flannery. 2. Salvation in literature.
3. Christianity in literature. 4. O'Connor, Flannery—
Pictorial works. 5. Southern States—Pictorial works.
6. Authors, American—20th century—Biography.
I. Gilbert, Douglas R., 1942-   . II. Title.
PS3565.C57Z6674 1986   813'.54   86-6339

ISBN 0-8028-0187-0 (pbk.)

List of Abbreviations

CS	*Flannery O'Connor: The Complete Stories.* New York: Farrar, Straus & Giroux, 1972.
M & M	*Mystery & Manners: Occasional Prose.* Ed. by Sally Fitzgerald and Robert Fitzgerald. New York: Farrar, Straus & Giroux, 1969.
VB	*The Violent Bear It Away.* New York: Farrar, Straus & Cudahy, 1960.
WB	*Wise Blood.* New York: 1952; rpt., Farrar, Straus & Cudahy, 1962.
Letters	*The Habit of Being: Letters of Flannery O'Connor.* Ed. Sally Fitzgerald. New York: Farrar, Straus & Giroux, 1979.

Table of Contents

Acknowledgments

The authors would like to thank the following for their help in the completion of this project. Mel Lorentzen of Wheaton College (Wheaton, Illinois) prepared the way for our research by writing a letter of introduction. Mary Fickett, the wife of the author of the text, performed the invaluable service of transforming the author's research notes into usable and beautifully organized files. Palmer and Alma Baker gave a generous grant that made the completion of the text possible. Mr. and Mrs. Jack W. McDonald of Griffin, Georgia, provided transportation and other logistical support to the authors while they were in Georgia. Gerald Becham, former Curator of the Flannery O'Connor Collection at the Ina Dillard Russell Library of Georgia College, and Robert M. Gorman, Coordinator of Information Services at the Ina Dillar Russell Library, provided access to the O'Connor Collection and guidance in our research. The Alumni Association of Georgia College was also most hospitable during our visit to Milledgeville. Sister Loretta of Our Lady of Perpetual Help Free Cancer Home in Atlanta and Father Paul of the Holy Spirit Monastery in Conyers gave us their time and insights into O'Connor's life. The authors also would like to thank the friends of O'Connor who have provided photographs of themselves for this volume.

The author of the text must acknowledge his debt to the biographical works on O'Connor that have preceded his. He has relied heavily on *Flannery O'Connor: Her Life, Library, and Book Reviews* by Lorine M. Getz, and the introductions to the various editions of O'Connor's work written by Sally Fitzgerald and Robert Fitzgerald. He has also benefited from the many articles published over the years in the *Flannery O'Connor Bulletin* which touch on aspects of O'Connor's life. Paul Engle, who founded the Writers Workshop at the University of Iowa, provided several key pieces of information. Anne Truitt, Acting Executive Director of Yaddo, and Kjersti Board, Assistant to the Archivist of Yaddo, were most helpful in specifying the dates of O'Connor's residence at Yaddo. Finally, I would like to thank my friends who have read and commented on the manuscript, and that generous authority who corrected a number of serious misimpressions.

The authors and the publisher wish to thank Harcourt Brace Jovanovich, Inc., and the Harold Matson Company, Inc., for permission to reprint brief excerpts from "The Displaced Person" and "A Temple of the Holy Ghost" by Flannery O'Connor. Copyright © 1953, 1954, 1955 by Flannery O'Connor.

We also wish to thank Farrar, Straus & Giroux, Inc., and the Harold Matson Company, Inc., for permission to reprint brief excerpts from the following works:

"Revelation" from *The Complete Stories* by Flannery O'Connor. Copyright © 1964, 1965 by Regina O'Connor.

"The Catholic Novelist in the Protestant South," "Novelist and Believer," "The Fiction Writer and His Country," and "Introduction to *A Memoir of Mary Ann*" from *Mystery and Manners* by Flannery O'Connor. Copyright © 1957, 1961, 1963, 1964, 1966, 1967, 1969 by the Estate of Mary Flannery O'Connor. Copyright © 1961 by Farrar, Straus & Cudahy, Inc.

The Habit of Being by Flannery O'Connor. Copyright © 1979 by Regina O'Connor.

The Violent Bear It Away by Flannery O'Connor. Copyright © 1955, 1960 by Flannery O'Connor.

Wise Blood by Flannery O'Connor. Copyright © 1949, 1952, 1962 by Flannery O'Connor.

The photographs in the text have been supplied by the following:

The Flannery O'Connor Collection, Ina Dillard Russell Library, Georgia College: 11, 12, 13, 14, 22, 24, 35, 39, 51, 88, 108

Douglas R. Gilbert: 21, 36, 37, 53, 82, 98, 109

Paul Engle: 29

Sally Fitzgerald: 31, upper left

Robert Giroux and Arthur W. Wang: 31, upper right

Rod Jellema: 31, bottom

Life and Work

Introduction

> One of the awful things about writing when you are a Christian is that
> for you the ultimate reality is the Incarnation, the present reality is the
> Incarnation, and nobody believes in the Incarnation; that is, nobody in
> your audience. My audience are the people who think God is dead. At
> least these are the people I am conscious of writing for.
>
> — Flannery O'Connor, *Letters*, p. 92

THE breakdown of the Christian consensus in Western civilization has proven to be very bad news for literature. We can start to see why by noting the advantages a writer of medieval times had over a writer today. Chaucer and his audience, unlike a contemporary author and his readership, shared an epic story or myth, the Christian faith. This common inheritance gave Chaucer a pattern for experience and the light by which to see it. The outline and the radiance of this story, which we might liken to a cathedral's rose window, were known; but each man's place, the segment his story would occupy in the great drama, was not. How that light refracted through each segment or pane, the color shed by a man's story, offered the writer a full spectrum of subject matter. Moreover, because the author and his audience shared the same faith, the author did not have to guess how his audience would judge people and incidents in his stories; his values were theirs. This allowed the author to concentrate wholly on bringing his narratives to life through the precision and grace of his poetry. As a result, the work of Chaucer and other medieval writers is imbued with a spirit of reconciliation, of being at home in this world although their preoccupations are otherworldly — a great paradox to the modern reader.

Our culture lacks a story with the mythic dimensions needed to unify it. The outline of what even well-educated people *should* know has been blurred past recognition by the many things we *can* know. In this situation, difficulties for the writer spring up like the fearsome army that came from the sowing of the dragon's teeth by Cadmus. The whole enterprise of literature has had to be reconsidered. How shall the writer understand his urge to create? How should the writer think of his function in society? And most importantly, can a central myth be replaced by anything else?

One question subsumes all the rest: If, at least in the sense of widespread unbelief, God is dead, is the creation of great literature possible?

The gargantuan works that were produced during the years of Modernism proper (ca. 1915-1941) attempted to provide new epics

1

whose revolutionary methods of construction would make great literature possible again, serving our time as the story of the gods served the ancient world and as Christianity served our culture before the Enlightenment. Although these works made use of some of the content of the old myths—and indeed were meant in part to provide access to these myths through reinterpretation—the governing genius of Modernist literature expressed itself in triumphs of form over content. The point of these works was the ingenious ways in which they were put together to the exclusion of any "moral" and over against even an experience of meaning. The problem was that the old myths were not only used but seemingly used up by methods that were so idiosyncratic as to resist imitation. Thus the great works of Modernism such as James Joyce's *Ulysses* and Ezra Pound's *Cantos* have not circumvented our need for a mythic background to our literature. Joyce's *Ulysses*, for example, casts a long and chilling shadow. Joyce imitated, parodied, and thus consumed the history of English prose style so well and above all so thoroughly that his feat can never be repeated. All fiction writers are now left to respond as best they can.

As a result of this mythic crisis, literature has turned in two directions. The first depends on the old myth of Christianity by reflecting on it in despair. Writers like Samuel Beckett have presented the horror of existence with a black humor that expresses the only courage possible for a creature—man—who through the cosmic accident of his creation has been endowed with the unique and useless ability to contemplate his own death. Beckett's *Waiting for Godot* sums up our condition in this fa-

mous and darkly clear phrase: "They give birth astride a grave, the light gleams an instant, then it's night once more." Nathanael West pushes black humor further—if that's possible—into the service of a searing nihilism. In West's *Miss Lonelyhearts* a young reporter begins to write the advice-to-the-lovelorn column. After reading the heartfelt letters of pathetically wretched people, he succumbs to despair. His hard-boiled boss, Shrike, razzes him unmercifully about his once-tender hopes. The older man catalogues the different possible modes of contemporary salvation, but he concludes they are all worthless:

> "My friend, I know of course that neither soil, nor the South Seas, nor hedonism, nor art, nor suicide, nor drugs, can mean anything to us. We are not men who swallow camels only to strain at stools. God alone is our escape. This church is our only hope, The First Church of Christ Dentist, where He is worshipped as Preventer of Decay. The church whose symbol is the trinity new-style: Father, Son and Wirehaired Fox Terrier. . . ."

Many contemporary writers, on the other hand, have taken refuge in manipulations of language for their own sake. Thus the elaborate gamesmanship of much modern and contemporary writing, the construction of Barth's "funhouses," halls of endlessly repeating mirrors, forming labyrinths in which we may lose ourselves for a time and forget—and perhaps find solace for—our predicament. Thus stories like "The Glass Mountain" from Donald Barthelme, which turns—reversing the order of criticism—a "beautiful enchanted symbol" into a princess in order to throw her and the literary tradition she represents off the top of a skyscraper. Thus Robert Coover's "The Babysitter," a story in which a middle-aged man's seduction of the family baby-sitter triumphs over its clichéd situation by anatomizing word-play that destroys the distinction between fantasy and reality.

Now the Christian who writes in our time — for indeed such a creature still exists — has some of the same advantages as Chaucer over his unbelieving colleagues. He does not have to create his own imaginative universe wholesale. He does not have to try to restructure the entire tradition of letters in the West by combing Provençal poetry and Chinese verse in order to present his culture with a new syllabus of what an educated man ought to have read, as Ezra Pound did. The writer who is a Christian can feel free to explore every facet of human experience in the knowledge that though we and our world have been marred by original sin, the Creator is still evident in creation, and God's fundamental evaluation of his world as "good" remains unchanged.

At the same time, the writer who is a Christian will, unfortunately, have to confront a reading public whose sensibilities have been formed by the last three centuries of unbelief, sensibilities that have not simply been changed but have been impaired as a result of secularism's triumph. He will have to take into account what T. S. Eliot called our "dissociation of sensibility," the separation that exists between reason and imagination, the gulf of skepticism that for most people effectively prevents the approach of grace to the limits of the natural world. Indeed, the category of the "real" has nearly been limited to empirically verifi-

able matters, and thus things invisible have been excluded a priori from literature that pretends to be "realistic." The Christian writer will have to consider that most people have long forgotten that physics was once considered a division of metaphysics. He will become aware that he is speaking to people whose grave suspicions, although they might not admit it, are those of Nathanael West. He will therefore face the challenge of making belief believable in a time, to paraphrase Eliot, that could not seem more unpropitious.

In the twentieth century, writers who are Christians have responded to our inbred agnosticism in two principal ways. One group has viewed the direction of modern and contemporary literature as a historical aberration; they have insisted that all cultures at all other times have at least had some notion of the sacred and have tried to follow this perception into a deeper experience of reality. As Christian humanists they have felt free to take a synthetic approach to the myths of all cultures, believing that they point to the ultimate and historical myth of Christianity. From these mythic sources and the tradition of Western literature during the ages of belief they have constructed new fictions. The myth-like fantasies of J. R. R. Tolkien, the space fictions of C. S. Lewis, and the supernatural thrillers of Charles Williams are good and sometimes great examples of what can be accomplished in this way. The work of these writers and others like them reopens the questions of metaphysics by positing fantastic worlds in which the supernatural is simply a given. They ask the reader to dwell in these spacious realms and, while experiencing the pleasure of these larger vistas, to consider whether these fabulous worlds are not, in truth, more like the "real" world than the reader had supposed.

Other writers with Christian visions have chosen to work within the genres and modes of modern and contemporary writing. These writers not only recognize the diminished range of perception and feeling among people today but acknowledge that this process has affected them, too. Fantasy literature does not attract them because their taste has to a large extent been formed, as has the reader's, by the modern world; and they must know instinctively, one supposes, that readers like themselves would either dismiss out-of-hand the questions of fantasy literature or miss entirely the deeper concerns of this kind of imaginative writing. This argument has merit. Tolkien, for example, was read widely and with great enthusiasm by young people in the late 1960s and 1970s; but most of these people would still be shocked to learn that Tolkien, far from being the most far-out of the mind-trippers, was a crusty Roman Catholic. This second group of writers insists, in fact, that if readers are deaf, dumb, and blind to spiritual reality, this in itself is a kind of negative testimony to the existence of God and his immanence in creation. As Binx, the main character in Walker Percy's *The Moviegoer*, notes,

REMEMBER TOMORROW

Starting point for search:

It no longer avails to start with creatures and prove God.

Yet it is impossible to rule God out.

The only possible starting point: the strange fact of one's own invincible apathy — that if the proofs were proved and God presented himself, nothing would be changed. Here is the strangest fact of all.

Abraham saw signs of God and believed. Now the only sign is that all the signs in the world make no difference. Is this God's ironic revenge? But I am onto him.

Writers in this group would include the poets T. S. Eliot, David Jones, and W. H. Auden, and the fiction writers François Mauriac, Georges Bernanos, Evelyn Waugh, Graham Greene, Walker Percy, Frederick Buechner, and the subject of this short life, Flannery O'Connor.

Twenty years have passed since Flannery O'Connor's death, and the growth of her audience and the critical industry devoted to examining her short stories and novels during this time stands as a sign that she was one of the greatest comic writers of the twentieth century. Her fictions are "comic" both in the formal, literary sense — they are informed by a vision of life as a divine comedy — and in the popular sense — they are very funny. The order of O'Connor's humor further distinguishes her from other great writers of her time. It does not, as in P. G. Wodehouse, derive from a retreat into a fanciful land of eccentric English manners and tastes where harsh realities are buffered by a Romantic dream of society, money, and incurable naiveté. Nor is it exactly like the black humor of Beckett, although there are moments in O'Connor's fictions when the irony becomes at once "funny because it is terrible, or . . . terrible because it is funny" (*Letters*, p. 105). O'Connor's humor arises from a sense of play, but one different from Barth's gamesmanship as well—it is neither born out of desperation nor saturated with futility. Not earthbound, it rises, an agent of transcendence as well as of the darker truths. Her humor has affinities with Chaucer's rambunctiousness, just as her beliefs shared an affinity with his. Her comedy was the measure of humanity's distance—the extent to which it had fallen—from its Creator. She wrote the way she did, she was even able to be funny in her inimitable way, because she was a Christian.

This might lead one to suppose that her faith provided a means of disregarding the horrors of our time, that she concentrated on the big picture of providence and, with her eyes uplifted to the final consummation of Redemption, was able to overlook what has stared the rest of us down: the trench warfare of the First World War, the Holocaust and the atomic bomb of the Second World War, and the triumph of totalitarianism in nation after nation. But this was not the case. The problem of evil did not lead her into despair or to the usual rationalizations of sentimental piety. She found no need, in a phrase she quoted from Baron von Hugel in his same tone of loathing, to "tidy-up reality." And neither did the rustic locales of her stories allow her any escape. As she pointed out, "It's well to remember that the serious fiction writer always writes about the whole world, no matter how limited his particular scene. For him, the bomb that was dropped on Hiroshima affects life on the Oconee River, and there's not anything he can do about it" (*M & M*, p. 77). Rather, Flannery O'Connor proceeded (as I noted my second group of Christian writers do) from a full rec-

ognition of the problems of the age and its anxious spirit. She wrote to one of her correspondents, "If you live today you breathe in nihilism. In or out of the Church, it's the gas you breathe" (*Letters*, p. 97). And to another she wrote, "I am a Catholic peculiarly possessed of the modern consciousness, that thing Jung describes as unhistorical, solitary, and guilty. To possess this within the Church is to bear a burden, the necessary burden for the conscious Catholic. It's to feel the contemporary situation at the ultimate level" (*Letters*, p. 90).

Many Christians anesthetize the pain in *Miss Lonelyhearts* by taking offense, but O'Connor did not. She was very much influenced by West, especially as a graduate student at the University of Iowa. She realized that he had found a way to express that nihilistic atmosphere, that he had created fictions that concurred with Nietzsche's prediction that the best thing about Western civilization—its relentless quest for the truth—would finally bring with it the worst possible news: the extent of man's corruption. O'Connor was thankful to skeptics like Camus, whose commitment to justice she took as a refining fire for her own faith.

This was no easy thing to do, of course. The pain of feeling "the contemporary situation at the ultimate level" comes through in lines she wrote to the novelist John Hawkes: "It's hard to believe always but more so in the world we live in now. There are some of us who have to pay for our faith every step of the way and who have to work out dramatically what it would be like without it and if being without it would be ultimately possible or not" (*Letters*, pp. 349-50). It is evident that her vocation as a writer and her faith were intimately connected. She understood quite clearly that the gift she had been given obliged her to work out her salvation, both personally and in terms of the authenticity of her fiction, in the constant awareness of what Beckett could only denominate as the "unnameable."

O'Connor, I'm sure, would at this point be very uncomfortable with having ascribed to her any special form of spiritual heroism, with the implication that she was a suffering servant for the world of belles lettres. She thought she'd finally get saved, but it would take a good long stay in purgatory to complete the process (*Letters*, p. 361). O'Connor saw herself as simply another Christian getting on with the tasks ahead of her, aided at every turn by the Roman Catholic Church and its dogmas. "If I hadn't had the Church to fight it [nihilism] with or tell me the necessity of fighting it," she wrote, "I would be the stinkingest logical positivist you ever saw right now" (*Letters*, p. 97). And shortly before she confessed to being possessed of that modern consciousness, she wrote, "I think that the Church is the only thing that is going to make the terrible world we are coming to endurable; the only thing that makes the Church endurable is that it is somehow the body of Christ and that on this we are fed" (*Letters*, p. 90).

That O'Connor did receive nourishment from that source can hardly be doubted. We have the undeniable evidence of transubstantiated experience in the stories themselves. And here we arrive at the dilemma that confronts her commentators. The reader can divorce an evaluation of her work from any consideration of her life. But the biographer cannot separate her spiritual growth from her growth as an artist. Just as her vocation, her work, leads us as readers into the mystery of Christ, so it often pointed the way in her private life as well. In being true to her as an artist, we will find ourselves obliged to assess her sanctity. Understanding this, we will want to see how her life affected her work and, in turn, how her work affected her life. Indeed, her vocation is the best starting point for our inquiry because it speaks of her essential identity, the union of her life and work.

The artistic task, O'Connor argued, always involves a descent into the depths of the self and thereby into the heart of experience. She was fond of quoting Joseph Conrad's statement that the artist "descends within himself, and in that region of stress and strife, if he be deserving and fortunate, he finds the terms of his appeal" (*M & M*, p. 196). She qualified this for herself by saying, "This descent into himself will, at the same time, be a descent into his region. It will be a descent through the darkness of the familiar world where, like the blind man cured in the gospels, he sees men as if they were trees, but walking" (*M & M*, pp. 49-50). Here Christ's healing of this blind man represents the healing of spiritual blindness through the form of prophecy, the enlivening of the imagination, that belongs to the artist. She liked this image of distorted vision for its layers of meaning, its sense of restoration, its provisional character — in the consummation of history we will "know as we are known" — and its implication that true sight may begin to come to us through faculties or a medium that must at first appear distorted. It gives us "eyes to see" reality, not in its essence but as it is hidden within people and events. It is not the form of prophecy given to Moses — God speaking directly to man — but the kind limited to the scent that triggers memory, to the phrase in conversation that lingers in the mind long after its context has been forgotten, to the Eliotian hints and guesses that awaken the imagination. And finally, because appearance and reality are not always the same, art will have to distort in order to reveal. In Picasso's phrase, art is a lie that tells the truth.

Again, this is not to say that the writer who is a Christian projects his own view of reality, for his own descent mirrors in little the action of God in creating the world. Explaining this, O'Connor referred to a passage from the greatest of the church fathers:

> St. Augustine wrote that the things of the world pour forth from God in a double way: intellectually into the minds of angels and physically into the world of things. To the person who believes this — as the western world did up until a few centuries ago — this physical, sensible world is good because it proceeds from a divine source. The artist usually knows this by instinct; his senses, which are used to penetrate the concrete, tell him so. When Conrad said that his aim as an artist was to render the highest possible justice to the visible universe, he was speaking with the novelist's surest instinct. The artist penetrates the concrete world in order to find at its depths the image of its source, the image of ultimate reality. (*M & M*, p. 157)

The believing writer's descent is not at all restricted, as his unbelieving counterpart often believes his to be, to a literary spelunker's ex-

ploration of the cave of the unconscious. Rather, as God pours himself out into the world of matter, the writer empties himself, escaping egocentricity as much as possible, and in becoming self-forgetful he finds the natural order a medium of communion with God.

The seal and bond of this communion is the union in one figure of God's emptying himself into creation and man's encounter with God in the concrete: the Christ. The Incarnation is both the signifier of this reality and what is signified, the reality itself. He is the "ultimate image" that the writer will discover if he looks long and hard enough. For the Incarnation is not only the "ultimate reality" but the "present reality" as well. He is "the divine milieu," as Teilhard de Chardin — a great visionary, in O'Connor's opinion — entitled one of his books. "For 'in him we live and move and have our being' " (Acts 17:28).

As a Christian humanist O'Connor had a very high view of natural revelation: she believed that the artist, if he is doing his job properly, can hardly fail to testify to the consequences of God becoming incarnate, even if only by way of presenting the destruction, the evil, where he is rejected.

The light of natural revelation grew immeasurably more intense in the revelation of Christ as manifested in his presence in the church, especially in the forms of the Eucharist, baptism, and the other sacraments. If the Eucharist was only a symbol, she blurted out once, then "to hell with it." The historical fact of the Incarnation and the timeless reality of his presence in the church and its sacraments were the touchstones of her belief. That matter in the body of Christ had been consecrated and raised up to heaven as the vessel of charity gave her the conviction that, despite the age of unbelief in which she lived, there must be points of contact between the holy and the secular world of modern man. If the holy is revealed to us through matter, then it must be possible to present it in a credible way through the matter of stories. "The real novelist," she wrote, "the one with an instinct for what he is about, knows that he cannot approach the infinite directly, that he must penetrate the natural human world as it is. The more sacramental his theology, the more encouragement he will get from it to do just that" (*M & M*, p. 163).

Her sacramental theology solved, at least in theory, our problem of dissociation of sensibility. The Incarnation guarantees that our apprehension of life as meaningful — including the categories (i.e., the sacred and the profane) and modes (through space and time) of perception — is, at least in an analogous sense, one with God's view of the world. The shadow that falls between life as we experience it (the phenomenal) and life as it is in itself (the noumenal) can be dissipated in the light of Christ. We do not have to opt for a literature of despair in which man's quest for meaning is seen as absurd, or a literature of gamesmanship in which we are constantly reminded that the symmetry or internal coherence of the works says nothing about the real world but only serves to increase our pleasure in reading. We can aim, O'Connor believed, for the revelation of truth. When her contemporaries were convinced that they were locked inside their own skulls, O'Connor found in the thought of Saint Thomas Aquinas an understanding of creativity that opened up the world to the artist and welcomed him:

> St. Thomas called art "reason in making." This is a very cold and very beautiful definition, and if it is unpopular today, this is because reason has lost ground among us. As grace and nature have been separated, so imagination and reason have been separated, and this always means an end to art. The artist uses his reason to discover an answering reason in everything he sees. For him, to be reasonable is to find, in the object, in the situation, in the sequence, the spirit which makes it itself. This is not an easy or simple thing to do. It is to intrude upon the timeless, and that is only done by the violence of a single-minded respect for the truth. (*M & M*, pp. 82-83)

Reason can hardly be very useful to people, especially artists, who believe that this faculty came into being by chance and that its propensity for discovering causal, symmetric, and harmonic relationships reveals its inutility; who think of reason as a Chinese lantern, projecting chimeras that either mask or devour the real, feeding the dragon of the intellect. The surrealists, holding this view, resorted to oblique means of creating in order to short-circuit the rational and make contact with the world-in-itself. O'Connor, instead of trying to subvert reason in order to unfetter the imagination, could embrace reason's very limitations as a means of transcending them and encountering the holy.

Since we are made in the image of God, the structures of reason must correspond to the Image after which they are patterned. His creation must also reflect this image and therefore can be our textbook on creativity: from it we learn to imitate the Creator's original action. At the same time, however, we will learn how in being creators we cannot be the Creator himself. We will see that we do not create out of nothing, *ex nihilo,* and that the symmetries of the universe are truly fearful in contrast to those we can bring into being. Our approach will entail humility. At this juncture, however, a paradoxical reversal takes place between the artist who believes and the one who does not. When the artist puts himself at the center of the universe, he longs for his imagination to be godlike and finds it absolutely earthbound — strictly limited, in fact, to the confines of the self. But the bond of faith leads the believing artist into an encounter with the strange, the fabulous, the awesome — with all those things that make God the Other. Through time we discover the timeless; through the natural, the supernatural. Few of us are up to such a pursuit, but the conditions of the encounter do not exclude anyone.

O'Connor's attempt to find "in the object, in the situation, in the sequence, the spirit which makes it itself" gave her a radically different view of content. She found in her faith the hope of incarnating "imaginative truth" in her work at a time when the imagination and truth were thought to have little to do with one another. She was well aware of how much her views differed from those of her colleagues and of the difference this made in their fictions:

> The novelist tries to give you, within the form of the book, a total experience of human nature at any time. For this reason the greatest dramas naturally involve the salvation or loss of the soul. Where there is no belief in the soul, there is very little drama. The Christian novelist is distinguished from his pagan colleagues by recognizing sin as sin. According to his heritage he sees it not as sickness or an accident of environment, but as a responsible choice of offense against God which involves his eternal future. Either one is serious about salvation or one is not. And it is well to realize that the maximum amount of seriousness admits the maximum of comedy. Only if we are secure in our beliefs can we see the comical side of the universe. One reason a great deal of contemporary fiction is humorless is because so many of these writers are relativists and have to be continually justifying the actions of their characters on a sliding scale of values. (*M & M,* pp. 167-68)

These days we are often prompted by many within the cultural establishment to think of sin and salvation as extraneous matters. But the literature of unbelief has, in its own way, been informed by these issues. What point does Sartre have to make that is more important, more crucial than his belief that *there is no such thing as human nature*? The greatest dramas still involve the salvation or loss of the soul. The loss of the soul, its very existence, howls through Beckett's dramas. Beckett is a writer who could not be more serious about salvation; his dramas are plays of salvation in which the hope of salvation is all but snuffed out. As to sin, Camus once defined alienation as evil without God. All these issues are absolutely pertinent to everything Nathanael West wrote. The pain the Miss Lonelyhearts columnist feels, for example, comes from being stuck with a diagnosis — religious hysteria — when what he wants is a vocation. O'Connor took these pagan colleagues seriously because they did know what was crucial; her work, though in no way departing from the requirements of art to evangelize, does constitute a reply to theirs. In this, as in her personal attitudes, she honored their integrity and artistry. And yet she could laugh about it all in a way impossible to them. Christianity is a strangely cheery religion. It knows the world wants to pitch itself into hell, is always in the act of doing just that. But, as the comic structures of O'Connor's fictions make clear, it also knows that nothing but an adamantine will can separate us from the love of Christ.

Mary Flannery

Flannery, age two, with her mother, Regina. In the letters she wrote as an adult, Flannery wryly referred to her mother as "the parent."

WHEN we refer to Flannery O'Connor as the author of *Wise Blood* and her other works, we have in mind not so much a person as a lasting image: the author has nearly become the substance and the attributes of her work, or the animating intelligence we find everywhere immanent in that work. This identification makes the life of the author seem as inevitable as the claims the work itself makes upon us. We think of *the* O'Connor as powerful, comic, visionary — and finished, perfected. There was nothing inevitable, however, about the life and career of Flannery O'Connor; paradoxically, only the unlikeliness of who she was and what she wanted to do explains, in part, her achievement — for only great art is capable of reconciling the disparate elements of her experience, her training, and the times in which she lived.

She was born Mary Flannery O'Connor on March 25, 1925, the only child of Edward Francis O'Connor, Jr., and Regina Cline O'Connor. Her parents came from families that were prominent in two of the major enclaves of Roman Catholic society within the fundamentalist environs of Georgia: the O'Connors were well-known in Savannah and the Clines in Milledgeville. Regina's family also had relatives in Savannah and visited there frequently. Her brother married a Savannah girl, and Regina met Edward O'Connor, the brother of the bride, at the wedding.

Flannery (right) giving a book close scrutiny at the tender age of three, and at seven (below), in a picture taken on the occasion of her First Communion.

The position of the O'Connors within the society of Savannah matched the central location of their home, which stands on the city square opposite the Cathedral of St. John the Baptist. Mary Flannery lived in this brownstone house for the first twelve years of her life. She was sent to St. Vincent's School, which was staffed by the Sisters of St. Joseph, and later briefly attended Sacred Heart High School.

Her father, whom she later referred to as Ed — just as she often called her mother by her first name — had served in the army as a lieutenant. He worked in real estate and was active in Savannah politics and the American Legion. Flannery's character was in many respects attributable to him. "I am never likely to romanticize him," she wrote to a close friend, "because I carry around most of his faults as well as his tastes" (*Letters*, p. 167). If she didn't romanticize him, she didn't discount the good in the man, either. "Last year," she wrote to the same correspondent, "I read over some of the speeches he made and was touched to see a kind of patriotism that most people would just laugh at now, something childlike, that was a good deal too good and innocent for the Legion" (*Letters*, p. 167). Ed encouraged his daughter's bent toward the arts by carrying around her first drawings and poems in order to show them to friends. He set her an example as well by writing those speeches and other occasional pieces. Looking back, Flannery thought Ed would have pursued writing seriously, as a vocation, if he had had the time or the money or the training that she received. What Flannery perceived as their mutual am-

Regina Cline O'Connor and Edward Francis O'Connor. Mr. O'Connor, whom Flannery mentioned with great tenderness in her letters, died of lupus in 1941, when Flannery was not quite sixteen.

bition prompted a confession formed by a depth of feeling and expressed in an unguarded way (most unusual to her) that makes her love for him transparent: "Whatever I do in the way of writing makes me extra happy in the thought that it is a fulfillment of what he wanted to do himself" (*Letters*, p. 167).

The character that was forming in this little girl in Savannah was dominated by two traits antagonistic to one another: she was at once highly sensitive and fiercely independent. Her childhood, by her own account and others, was unusually happy. Yet as she approached adolescence these two traits combined to make her a solitary figure, extremely private, and, later on, shy. In an early notebook Flannery

kept when she was twelve, she posted this warning to unwanted readers on the first page: "I know some folks that don't mind thier own bisnis" (*Letters*, p. xi). Her sensitivity can be discerned in retrospect through a comment she made about her father. "He needed the people I guess and got them. Or rather wanted them and got them. I wanted them and didn't. We are all rather blessed in our deprivations if we let ourselves be, I suppose" (*Letters*, p. 169). In the immediate context she is referring to the isolation imposed upon her by her illness, but her feelings in this matter seem to me indicative of an acute longing that began early. She had the more than ample heart of someone who is shy.

But her independent nature was so strong that, as much as she might have liked being popular with her elders or some of her peers, she couldn't help but be herself and go her own way. In her girlhood this even extended to her relations with the celestial powers. The nuns at her parochial school had informed her that every child has a guardian angel, and from the time she was eight until she was twelve, she practiced what she later termed "anti-angel aggression":

> It was my habit to seclude myself in a locked room every so often and with a fierce (and evil) face, whirl around in a circle with my fists knotted, socking the angel. . . . My dislike of him was poisonous. I'm sure I even kicked at him and landed on the floor. You couldn't hurt an angel but I would have been happy to know I had dirtied his feathers — I conceived of him in feathers. (*Letters*, pp. 131-32)

The inherent tensions in her nature were borne in upon her by a precociously high degree of self-consciousness — that presiding spirit of reflection characteristic of writers. This trait, which gave her a certain distance from events or, as Hawthorne called it, "ice in the blood," would enable her to see her experience clearly enough to remake it into fiction; but it would also alienate her from the blessed state of being wholly present in one's actions, coincident with them, at home in the present tense. She showed an intuitive grasp of cliché and irony by bringing a tomato, instead of an apple, to her teacher. At twelve she decided she would not get any older. "There was something about 'teen' attached to anything," she wrote later, "that was repulsive to me. I certainly didn't approve of

Flannery at twelve. In a reminiscence she noted, "I was a very ancient twelve. . . . I am much younger now than I was at twelve or anyway, less burdened. The weight of the centuries lies on children, I'm sure of it."

what I saw of people that age. I was a very ancient twelve; my views at that age would have done credit to a Civil War veteran" (*Letters*, pp. 136-37). She's laughing at herself here, but that shouldn't lead us to dismiss the insight of Mary Flannery at twelve. If she didn't know that adolescence and early adulthood would bring with them compensations, she did know why every poet has spoken of love as a form of madness, and sex, with which the teenager's body forces him to be preoccupied, as ludicrous. She knew she was going to have to cope with forces so powerful that even someone with a will as strong as hers would be made to look a fool by them. And what could be more painful for someone with that much pride and sensitivity than watching herself give way with a terrible detachment?

Mary Flannery dealt with her own particular slant on the difficulties of growing up in two notable ways. She developed what she terms, in an autobiographical piece she wrote while she was in graduate school at Iowa, a "you-leave-me-alone-or-I'll-bite-you complex." By asserting the abrasive side of her personality, she found out quickly who could love her for herself, and at the same time, with the genius of the subconscious, she fended off contact with those whose love she would never win anyway. Flannery also began collecting domesticated birds — chickens, ducks, and geese — which led eventually to her fascination with peacocks.

At the age of five she was given a pet bantam chicken that could walk backwards as well as forwards. The Pathé News service sent out a team of reporters and photographed and filmed the child with her freakish pet. The story appeared in the nation's newspapers, and the filmed version found its way into the newsreels of the time. Flannery's collection of birds grew through the years, and always she was on the lookout for the exotic among such fowl. This only child, sensitive and independent, must have found needed companions in her collection of birds, but there must have been more to it as well. That a writer who would one day produce sometimes bizarre stories cultivated this taste for the exotic from an early age has given rise to a great deal of psycho-

logical speculation. Indeed, stories like "A Temple of the Holy Ghost" invite this kind of speculation.

In this short story, two teenage girls, Joanne and Susan, leave the convent where they attend high school to visit their great-aunt and her twelve-year-old daughter on their farm. The twelve-year-old is never named but called simply "the child" throughout the story. She's a dead ringer for Mary Flannery at that age: she wants to be friends with the older girls (she "wants the people"), but since they have come together she knows they will remain wrapped up in each other: "She was out of it and watched them suspiciously from a distance" (*CS*, p. 236). When Joanne and Susan go out to a fair with two neighbor boys, the child thinks that she would have refused to go with them anyway, even if they had asked her, an instance of sour grapes that reveals the sensitive side of her nature. The outlandish and obstreperous side is there as well. During dinner she laughs so hard at one of her own jokes that she falls backwards out of her chair and rolls on the floor laughing. And when one of the boys who is to take the girls to the fair mistakes the girls' rendition of *Tantum Ergo Sacramentum* for "Jew singing," the child cannot help screaming, "You big dumb Church of God ox!" (*CS*, p. 241).

It is always hazardous to speculate that a character represents a portrait of the author and then read what happens to the character back into the author's own life — formalist critics would consider this procedure anathema. And surely I admit that even if this character does closely resemble Mary Flannery at the watershed age of twelve, O'Connor was writing a story, not autobiography, and therefore everything in "A Temple of the Holy Ghost" — the elements of exaggeration and burlesque as well as the autobiographical refractions — serves the end of the story: an experienced meaning. Nevertheless, going about things this way, however heterodox, can be valuable. It's impossible for me to escape the conclusion that this story represents the way in which O'Connor herself came to read her own childhood, with a depth of recognition that lets us follow her imaginative descent and find with her the terms of her appeal. In another story the generic designation of the protagonist as "the child" might be used to present a character as typical; here it strikes me as a guilty admission that the child could have borne only one name — the author's own — or, as it stands, none at all.

When Joanne and Susan return from the fair, they reveal to the child that they have seen a hermaphrodite in one of the freak-show tents. Throughout the weekend the older girls have been preoccupied with their newfound sexuality. They call each other "Temple One" and "Temple Two" as a private joke. Its source, they finally explain to their great aunt and the child, is Sister Perpetua at their school: the nun has advised her charges that they should repulse any backseat overtures by saying, "Stop sir! I am a Temple of the Holy Ghost!" (*CS*, p. 238). The girls would relish any such encounter, of course, as long as it didn't carry any real threat. But while they are delighted to dip their toes and wade in the sexual shallows, their short encounter with the hermaphrodite, with the icy currents of the depths, sends a chill through them, dampening their enthu-

siasm and sending them back with relief, we feel, to the convent.

Although she has only secondhand knowledge of the freak, the child proves to have an imaginative capacity that makes the hermaphrodite more present for her than the older girls allow him to be for them; he is an "answer to a riddle that was more puzzling than the riddle itself" (*CS*, p. 245). The older girls are preoccupied with the riddle, sexuality, but the child is taken up with the puzzling reality of the hermaphrodite and in her own way puzzles out his meaning. When he appears before the crowds in his tent, the hermaphrodite says, "God made me thisaway and if you laugh He may strike you the same way. This is the way He wanted me to be and I ain't disputing His way. I'm showing you because I got to make the best of it" (*CS*, p. 245). In the child's sleepy imaginings that same night, the words of the hermaphrodite come back, but the tent setting is transformed into that of a church. The hermaphrodite praises God for the way God has made him. "Raise yourself up. A temple of the Holy Ghost. You! You are God's temple, don't you know? Don't you know? God's Spirit has a dwelling in you, don't you know?" The crowd responds, in an antiphonal manner, with cries of "Amen." But the antiphonal structure of assertion and response is broken toward the end as the child begins to drift off to sleep. The last statement, "I am a temple of the Holy Ghost," occurs in the place of a congregational response, and the breakdown of the dialectic lets the statement stand as equally applicable to the freak, everyone in the imagined crowd, and the child herself (*CS*, p. 246).

When the child and her mother take the

girls back to the convent, Mount St. Scholastica, they are invited to come to the evening service of Benediction, in which Christ's presence in the Host is adored. The child's independent spirit is chafed by the ready affection of the nuns and their childlike enthusiasm for this dramatic service. But finally, during the singing of the *Tantum Ergo Sacramentum,* as the Benediction progresses,

> her ugly thoughts stopped and she began to realize that she was in the presence of God. Hep me not to be so mean, she began mechanically. Hep me not to give her so much sass. Hep me not to talk like I do. Her mind began to get quiet and then empty but when the priest raised the monstrance with the Host shining ivory-colored in the center of it, she was thinking of the tent at the fair that had the freak in it. The freak was saying, "I don't dispute hit. This is the way He wanted me to be." (*CS*, pp. 247-48)

This passage must be read in the light of another. Earlier in the story the child is reminded of how the freak tents at last year's fair — which she did attend on a special day for children — inspired in her the ambition to become a doctor. Reviewing her current ambition to become an engineer, she grows dissatisfied. She imagines the revolving searchlight of the fair, the place itself "raised up in a kind of gold sawdust light" (*CS*, p. 242), and she yearns for a better destiny, something braver, more consuming, and inclusive. "She would have to be a saint," she decides, "because that was the occupation that included everything you could know; and yet she knew she would never be a saint." She does believe that "she

could be a martyr if they killed her quick" (*CS*, p. 243). She envisions the course of her martyrdom, how the lions unleashed upon her would fall down at her feet, and how she would prove impossible to burn, and then her head would be cut off — very quickly. Her moment of epiphany while the Host is on exposition in the center of the sunburst monstrance indicates what the true nature of her martyrdom will be. Like the freak, like everyone, she exhibits the effects of original sin. She will not be ushered completely into the Lord's presence before her willfulness and pride die — not a quick death, probably, but the slow death of pride that the lifetime of any Christian entails. In order for her to be at last a worthy temple of the Holy Ghost, a monstrance of Christ's presence, she must cooperate with the Holy Spirit in making her soul a fit place for his habitation: the freakish imperfections of that temple must be righted by the Carpenter's joinery. And yet this is possible only if she accepts her defects and limitations, as the freak does ("I don't dispute hit"), and lifts up these things, her mere flesh, to God. For in the monstrance she sees the image of a God who both ascended, taking that flesh into heaven, as well as descended into this freakish world. The sins that beset the child can be transformed into the virtues that may participate in the salvation of the adult.

O'Connor once said, as I noted earlier, "We are all rather blessed in our deprivations if we let ourselves be." We cannot say this in other than her wistful tone, because it would obviously be less of a savaging nuisance to be back in Eden or translated directly into Paradise, but in making this affirmation, we may glimpse the painful love and even the humor of God. He seems to operate like the nun who says good-bye to the child at the convent door, who "swooped down on her mischievously and nearly smothered her in the black habit, mashing the side of her face into the crucifix hitched onto her belt" (*CS,* p. 248). Making us one with him, He impresses our own fates with his universal sacrifice. He imbues this world with his presence, making each person and event a sign of how we are to arrive at his Cross, a truth suggested by the last line of the story: "The sun was a huge red ball like an elevated Host drenched in blood and when it sank out of sight, it left a line in the sky like a red clay road hanging over the trees" (*CS,* p. 248). O'Connor knows at the end that the child's path, her path in growing up, was ordered as much as the sun's decline and was as saturated with God's presence. The beauty of the literary coda here seems the author's expression of praise and gratitude for this. For, as in the *Tantum Ergo Sacramentum,* "Faith, our outward sense befriending / Makes our inward vision clear."

I have prolonged the discussion of this story beyond its merely biographical significance in order to establish my own terms of appeal. Many readers are at first put off by O'Connor's work. The hermaphrodite is only one of the many freaks that appear in her work, and perhaps it's the easiest to take, since we are asked to identify first with the child and then through her with the hermaphrodite. But much of the concern about these freaks, especially the critical ballyhoo about the grotesque, is beside the point. This may have something to do with the status of Christianity in our society. A portion of our culture has become so post-Christian that religious allegiance startles them. Indeed, when, in 1957, O'Connor first published an essay in which she made clear her allegiance to orthodox Christianity, segments of the literary community were stunned — this writer whom they highly esteemed took redemption seriously? Many had seen nothing in her treatment of spiritual concerns but deflating irony and satire. The Christian world, on the other hand, has made Jesus such a housepet that when his true nature as the Lion of Judah is made manifest, the church scratches its head and doesn't know what to think. Another writer once commented that for all the talk about the inscrutable nature of the Eastern religious mind, the presence on any given Sunday morning of a hardware dealer in a Baptist church worshiping a God who became man and arose from the dead was far more inscrutable, bewildering, and strange than anything in Eastern spirituality. From God's point of view, as we understand it through church doctrine, a world suffering the effects of sin is way out of kilter; its normative state is perfection, and therefore the Christian above all should see the freakish aspects of life in the interregnum, in these last days, between Christ's first advent and his second coming. O'Connor did just that, and in using manifestly freakish images such as the hermaphrodite, she was trying to be unmistakably clear, not subtle in a falsely sophisticated way. "Never overlook the obvious" should be the first axiom of any critical approach to her work.

That said, the child in "A Temple of the Holy Ghost" demonstrates that she possesses the gift of imaginative prophecy in inchoate form, the gift that O'Connor herself possessed and developed. The child's courage in facing a dark aspect of experience and her startling imagination, which she uses to pierce its meaning, are essential to O'Connor's genius.

Because of this gift and the sensitivity and inexplicable conduct that came with it, Mary Flannery must have had a sense, as the child does in the story, of being odd man out, freakish. At this point we have to be careful to remain faithful both to the story and to the objective circumstances of Mary Flannery's life. The point of having the child identify with the hermaphrodite in the story is that everyone, from the normal twelve-year-old girl brought up in a proper family to the hermaphrodite, is in one and the same respect freakish: each of us suffers from the corruption of nature brought about by the Fall. Even if we are seemingly whole in body and mind, the kind of alienation from the self that we see in the child, the war of irrational impulses against lofty aspirations, afflicts us all. The only thing that singles out the child as an unusual person is her ability to see this.

Mary Flannery had a normal and happy childhood. But the conflicts in her emotional life, the difficulties that grew out of her being at once so independent and yet so sensitive, would later give her an important key to the freakishness of human nature. She seems to have first expressed her own sense of this freakishness through her love of exotic birds. Her initial atttraction to them may have meant little, but its development, its cultivation, has to stand as a correlative of Mary Flannery's inner life. One of the moving things about "A Temple of the Holy Ghost" is that we can see O'Connor looking back at herself as a twelve-year-old and shaping this portrait in accord with what necessarily remained hidden from her as a child: the secret that God would use her early emotional struggles, as he would also use the deprivations brought on by her illness, to make her into the writer she became. The conflicts in her own personality became a means by which she would learn to identify with the impaired, the outcast, and the poor. And through this identification she would see, at last, the "ultimate image of reality," the Christ who himself went beyond identification to become, in actuality, impaired, outcast, and poor. Mary Flannery, burdened with her obstreperous nature, her sensitivity, and her self-consciousness, could never know that one day she would be able to write and affirm with joy, "His [the writer's] prophet-freak is an image of himself" (*M & M*, p. 118).

*   *   *

In 1938 O'Connor's father, Ed, was diagnosed as having disseminated lupus, a disease in which the immune system produces antibodies that attack the victim's own tissues. He would suffer from the disease over the next three years and die on February 1, 1941, about two months before Mary Flannery's sixteenth birthday. With the first attack he was no longer able to carry on his business, and the family decided to move to Milledgeville, Georgia, back to the house that Regina had grown up in, a home that her father had purchased in 1886.

The name Milledgeville isn't familiar to most Americans, yet it once had a prominent place in the nation's life: it was the state capital of Georgia until 1868. It remained an important city to the state's Roman Catholics, a sister enclave to Savannah's Catholic society. O'Connor's people on her mother's side played important roles in founding, nurturing, and giving leadership to this enclave, and were also influential in the life of the city as a whole. In 1886 Peter Cline, O'Connor's maternal grandfather, bought what had been the governor's mansion. Holding court there, he served as mayor of the town for twenty-two years thereafter. He married Kate L. Treanor, with whom he had seven children. When she died, he took her sister as a bride, and had nine children with her, the seventh among them being Mary Flannery's mother, Regina. The Treanors were in large part responsible for the gathering of Catholics in Milledgeville in the first place. The father of the women Peter Cline married, Hugh Treanor, who was Mary Flannery's maternal great-grandfather, held the first celebration of the mass in the city's history at his apartment in the Newell Hotel in 1874. His wife later donated the land for the church in which Mary Flannery worshiped most of her life.

Upon first inspection the move from Savannah to Milledgeville might appear disadvantageous to Mary Flannery's future career. Savannah was the more cosmopolitan city; there, her father, if he had remained in good health, would no doubt have continued to encourage her in her artistic ambitions and insured that Savannah's cultural resources were made available to her. More importantly, the Catholic community in Savannah was larger and better established than that in Milledgeville: its cohesiveness made a more relaxed at-

titude toward its Protestant neighbors possible. But it was the more intensely focused sense of place in Milledgeville, its thoroughly Southern identity, that proved of greater benefit to Mary Flannery in the long run. In Milledgeville she came to understand in detail the expression of the rural South's values in its manners. Her mother's people, the Treanor-Clines, were at the heart of the town's society. Mary Flannery was thus thrust into social situations — receptions, teas, and parties — that called upon her to act the Southern belle as well as she was able. Caught up in the life of the town, she was in an ideal position to observe Southern culture, with its hierarchical structure and its alien religion. She was forced to live out the ironic disjunctures of being a Catholic among Protestants — some of them, at the periphery of her world, fanatical. She began to face the central predicament of her life: what does the life of faith look like? Savannah contained one set of images, Milledgeville quite another.

Mary Flannery was enrolled in Peabody High School — the town lacked a parochial school at that level, so her parents had no other choice short of sending her away to school. Although remembrances of her at this age usually concern things she did alone rather than with friends, she was starting to leave behind some of her earlier introspection and channel that energy outward. She was writing short books about daily life — one entitled "My Relitives" (sic) — that she described as too old for children and too young for adults. She was also drawing and painting. Having submitted her cartoons to magazines, she cited "collecting rejection slips" as her hobby in her senior yearbook. Peabody was a progressive school, a

The Cline house, where the O'Connors lived after moving to Milledgeville in 1938.

Deweyan forerunner of the "free schools" of the 1960s and 1970s. In her later comments about it O'Connor disdained its brand of education: she felt that a classical education would have better prepared her to write.

In 1942 she entered Georgia State College for Women (now coed and called Georgia College). She much preferred the demands it placed upon her. These were the war years, and she kept at her studies year round, which enabled her to graduate a year early. She initially chose English as her major, but then changed to social science. This is perhaps the greatest irony in this master-of-irony's life: in her work she would satirize the relativism of the social sciences when she wasn't convicting them of being in league with the devil outright. While she was regarded as an eccentric in high

school — a girl who made a frock coat and trousers for a bantam chicken in home economics class — she came into her own in college. She had that happy experience of many intellectuals who, having endured the martial world of high school, find the reflective atmosphere of the university their element and, without the former Laocoön struggle of pubescence, rise to prominence, even leadership. Mary Flannery worked as the art editor of the student newspaper, *The Colonnade*, in which her cartoons appeared regularly. They were rather like those of Ogden Nash — all outline, with counterpoint in the background. She signed them with her initials, M. F. O., fashioned into the figure of a bird. She was also editor of *The Corinthian*, the college's literary quarterly, and the feature editor of her senior

Editor O'Connor, flanked by her staff, reviewing work on The Corinthian, *the literary quarterly of Georgia State College.*

yearbook. The college's faculty elected her to the Phoenix Society, its version of Phi Beta Kappa, during the fall quarter of her senior year, which tells us that she was in the top seven percent of her class.

The materials from her college years in the Flannery O'Connor Collection at Georgia College reveal more about her progress as a writer, in terms of both her technical facility and her sensibilities, than does this list of accomplishments. These papers show us the human being struggling with the language and what O'Connor, even toward the end of her life, termed her "poverty of means" to create. Rimbaud and Keats are the closest literary equivalents to Mozart in terms of early artistic development, and yet they produced their first recognized works in early adulthood, not in childhood. It takes a long time to make a writer, especially a writer of fiction as opposed to a poet. Mary Flannery's freshman composition papers are filled with overwriting, a trait endemic to the compositions of young people who love the language but don't yet know how to woo it. A single excerpt makes the point:

> His eyes canvassed the assemblage of loud-labeled tin cans, weighing down the insubstantial shelves than [sic] lined the wall. The sun, shinning [sic] through the skylight on them made the colors bounce before his astigmatic eyes like a galaxy of Indian notables, screaming and jumping through a war dance.

Poor diction, uneven tone, mixed metaphor, unneeded adjectives, bad spelling. She had a lot to learn—or unlearn.

The best of her college stories might be "The Coat," a kind of de Maupassant piece in which a black woman causes the death of her husband by making him hide the evidence of a crime he didn't commit. With the possible exception of its violent ending, this story shares little if anything with O'Connor's later writing. In this and other early stories characters reflect only occasionally on the essential questions that inform her mature work. Most of the time O'Connor is simply trying to get a character down. And although her ear for dialogue isn't bad, it does tend to err on the side of Br'er Rabbit.

What does seem in place from the very beginning, even in her childhood and high-school pieces, is her sense of humor, which brings with it an innately conservative skepticism. An example is found in a draft of a never-finished college essay about the typical chapel speaker's optimism concerning O'Connor's generation and the improvements they would surely bring about in the world:

> Apparantly [sic], in the eyes of the usual speaker youth carries with it all the qualities of interest, activeness, and that dauntless courage which will lead us into a sun of our own manufacture. Obviously, he should stick around awhile and see our duplicate copies of Uncle Bonah and Aunt Euphegia or the wavering products of uncertainty. What each is going to do to the future will not be one thousandth of what the future is going to do to each.

Another trait also surfaced early. The liveliest characters in the college stories tend to be those figures at the periphery of her world — she's drawn to them already. A fragment of a story has three boys who are ineligible for the draft riding around in a car, which makes one think immediately of Hazel and Enoch in *Wise Blood*. "The Coat" and this fragment do show that Mary Flannery had eliminated many of the weaknesses of her freshman compositions.

Although Mary Flannery was interested in writing from her high school years on, one of her teachers actually took the initiative in submitting some of her stories from *The Corinthian* to the graduate school at the State University of Iowa (now the University of Iowa). This school is known for being the home of the leading creative writing program in the country, the Writers Workshop. Mary Flannery would eventually become one of that program's most celebrated alumna. Yet she did not apply directly to the Writers Workshop. Her admittance, when it came, was to the graduate program in journalism. This suggests that as of the application deadline she was not sure, despite her collegiate endeavors, whether she should devote herself entirely to writing fiction.

But soon after she decided to go to Iowa, she had a talk with her mother that indicates that she was seeing the future more clearly. (Perhaps she had made up her mind to transfer, if she could, from the journalism program to the Writers Workshop.) She asked her mother whether outside of the family, for professional purposes, she might drop the use of her double name and be called simply "Flannery." Double names are common in the South, particularly combinations that affix a second name to "Mary," like "Mary Anne" and "Mary Frances." Outside of the South, however, the young writer must have feared that "Flannery" would be taken for her middle name, and only "women's writers" of sentimental fiction went by their full names. O'Connor knew enough about the direction of her work—even if she didn't have full confidence in its success—to know that for her to give the least impression of being one of these writers would amount to false advertising. She could have dropped "Flannery," of course, but "Mary O'Connor" may have seemed too nondescript. (Another writer, Mary McCarthy, would have to demonstrate how little there can be in a name.) And so she dropped the use of "Mary," and the writer, Flannery O'Connor, was born.

This discussion about what name she would use also illumines the lives of both mother and daughter and their relationship. It speaks of both their similarities and their differences. Regina and Flannery were forever turning away from one another and forever returning to each other like interlocked wheels in a timepiece; their worlds were in many respects entirely separate and yet touched each other at every point along the circumference of their lives. Flannery once wrote to a correspondent, "I always thought that if she [Regina] had a dog she'd name him Spot—without irony. If I had a dog, I'd name him Spot, with irony. But for all practical purposes no one would know the difference" (*Letters*, p. 236).

Flannery must have been nervous the day she and her mother discussed the matter of her writing. If she suspected what the nature of her fiction would be, then, in explaining that she did not want to be confused with the Margaret Mitchells of the world, she would have had to give Regina more than a vague impression of the direction in which her work was

Flannery in her college years. The level, determined gaze never changed.

heading. At first this was an abundant source of anxiety to her. In a letter to John Lynch, a fellow writer, she said, "I once had the feeling I would dig my mother's grave with my writing . . . , but I later discovered this was vanity on my part. They [mothers and other relatives] are hardier than we think" (*Letters*, p. 139). At the time of their talk Flannery didn't have any idea how hardy, how redoubtable, her mother would prove to be; but she did know that her mother would never understand or at least appreciate her kind of fiction very much. Perhaps her hesitance, as late as her senior year, to commit herself fully to a career of writing fiction stemmed in part from misgivings about her mother's reaction.

Neither woman could know the weight their relationship would bear in the coming years. The decision about what name Flannery would use and all that it signified was a first test of a bond that would have to hold firm when much greater trials came.

It would be only five-and-a-half years before Flannery contracted lupus, the same disease that killed her father. As a result, she would return from the North to Milledgeville and her mother. Regina would set up housekeeping at Andalusia, the farm she had inherited, and there nurse Flannery off and on for thirteen years. Their discussion of Flannery's new name was atypical; ordinarily their relationship had little to do with talking things out. The two women knew that ineradicable differences existed in their natures. Regina was social in the way of someone who enjoys the diversion; Flannery was more gregarious as she matured, but she still looked to a smaller circle of friends with whom she could be intimate. Flannery liked the kind of stories she wrote; Regina could barely get through Flannery's work, preferring, in Flannery's words, books with a lot of adventure and wild animals in them.

Regina's unstinting labor, care, and love should not be overlooked. Flannery's need would be obvious, and Regina not only responded but did so in a manner that made Flannery's professional life possible. Her conduct is even more admirable when we consider how many expectations her destiny undermined. She was the seventh of nine children, but she bore only one child. Her father must have seemed nearly immortal, an Old Testament patriarch blessed in the wealth of his family; Regina's husband died young. She had the aspirations of the rest of her family: to be a good and accomplished person in a good town, enjoying the fruits of her labors. But she ended up with a daughter who had outsized ambitions and interests, who was never on her own for long, and whose bewildering success brought all kinds of people to Regina's door as if she were the keeper of a shrine — people whose conversation, when she played hostess, often bored her. In many respects she was asked to give over her life to her child. And she did exactly that, without complaint.

For her part, Flannery recognized the differences between them and tried not to ask of Regina that she share her perspective. In the main she succeeded, but there was friction. In a letter to Cecil Dawkins, a fellow writer, she said,

> Your sale to the *Post* ought to impress your mother greatly. It sure has impressed my mother who brought the post card home. The other day she asked me why I didn't try to write something that people liked instead of the kind of thing I do write. Do you think, she said, that you are really using the talent God gave you when you don't write something that a lot, a LOT, of people like? This always leaves me shaking and speechless, raises my blood pressure 140 degrees, etc. All I can ever say is, if you have to ask, you'll never know. (*Letters*, p. 326)

She couldn't help hoping for more sympathy from her mother; no child can help longing for this, whatever age he or she attains. But Flannery was realistic, and she did her best to oil the machinery when the two wheels weren't meshing smoothly. To her good friend Maryat Lee she wrote,

> The only people of whom you can demand honesty are those you pay to get it from. . . .

Never, above all things, ask your *family* to be honest with you. This is putting a strain on the human frame it can't bear. [A person's] honesty is only honesty, not truth, and it can't be of much value to you intellectually or otherwise. To love people you have to ignore a good deal of what they say while they are being honest, because you are not living in the Garden of Eden any longer. (*Letters*, p. 283)

After Flannery had accepted the restrictions that lupus would impose on her life, she told her friend and biographer, Sally Fitzgerald, that one fear alone persisted: that her mother would die before she did (*Letters*, p. xii). She knew how much she depended on Regina, emotionally as well as physically. After their first important talk about her career, Flannery went off to Iowa, but she wrote her mother every day during the following years she spent away from Milledgeville.

The Young Writer

IN the fall of 1946 Flannery began her work at Iowa. Her first meeting with Paul Engle, the director of the Writers Workshop, was an encounter so entirely unpropitious that it smacks of the author's own sense of ironic providence. Flannery came into Engle's office and tried to explain who she was and what she was there for. But her heavy Southern accent prevented Engle from understanding a word she said, and he had to ask her to write down what she wanted. Engle says that Flannery wrote, "My name is Flannery O'Connor. I am not a journalist. Can I come to the Writer's Workshop?" He told her she should bring him samples of her work and, late as it was, they would consider her (*CS*, p. vii).

Soon the teacher and his new student were on speaking terms. Engle admired her work, and respected her willingness to accept criticism and rewrite pieces in the light of what she had learned. She must have found the competitive setting daunting, however. (In a writing workshop the teacher usually has a student read his or her piece, then leads a group discussion of it — a harrowing procedure, as anyone who has been through it knows.) Her fears conquered her normally combative manner, and shyness prevented her from reading her work aloud. But Engle was glad to render her the service of reading her stories himself. He recalls that once a guest writer, Robert Penn Warren, criticized a scene between a white man and a black man, and straightaway Flannery changed it. Commenting on her blend of shyness and tenacity, Engle has said,

"Flannery always had a flexible and objective view of her own writing, constantly revising, and in every case improving. The will to be a writer was adamant; nothing could resist it, not even her own sensibility about her own work. Cut, alter, try it again. . . . Sitting at the back of the room, silent, Flannery was more of a presence than the exuberant talkers who serenade every writing-class with their loudness. The only communicating gesture she would make was an occasional amused and shy smile at something absurd. The dreary chair she sat in glowed." (*CS*, pp. vii-viii)

Flannery claimed that she had never read much until she went to Iowa. Her college record shows this to be an overstatement. But it is true that she hadn't read as widely nor with the critical skills she gained at Iowa. The testy remarks she makes in *Mystery & Manners* about teachers of literature avoiding their proper subject by teaching cultural history reflect the change in approach between her college and graduate studies. The prime question of a beginning fiction writer is, What makes a story work? What makes a story in itself a good story? Cultural or intellectual history hardly addresses this question. Using the formalist text *Understanding Fiction* by Cleanth

Brooks and Robert Penn Warren, Flannery's professors at Iowa taught her what makes stories work by teaching her to read a story so closely that it finally, as if of itself, rendered up its meaning; they taught her to rely solely on the keys found within the story itself to interpret it. At Iowa she learned how to read in such a rewarding way that it seemed to her that she had never really read before. Her new skills enabled her to find the writers whose work would provide guidance for her own. She discovered that she was the spiritual heir of Nathaniel Hawthorne. Her enthusiasm for Henry James began. She journeyed through the works of Joseph Conrad, whose influence persisted and grew as she explored his entire corpus in later years. She learned the mandatory lessons that James Joyce has to teach. And she discovered her unbelieving counterpart: Nathanael West.

Her first efforts to get her stories published met with some success. *Accent* published "The Geranium" in 1946. Almost immediately the Ina Dillard Russell Library at Georgia College started collecting her published work and the stories about her that appeared in various publications. This gesture of pride turned out to be amazingly farsighted: it led to the establishment of the Flannery O'Connor Collection, a central bank for O'Connor's manuscripts and, eventually, for some of her effects, including her personal library.

After two years in residence at Iowa, Flannery received the master of fine arts degree in 1947. Her thesis consisted of her first six stories, published posthumously in *Flannery O'Connor: The Complete Stories*. Entitled *The Geranium: A Collection of Short Stories*, the thesis contains the work of a writer who has learned to think in prose. The writing is clean and competent; the transitions are graceful. The author's gift for simile highlights the stories with moments of sudden beauty. But the distinctive vision of the mature Flannery O'Connor is absent.

"The Geranium" is about the lost identity of an old Southerner who should never have accepted his daughter's invitation to live with her in New York. In retrospect, the figure of the old man suggests something of the mature O'Connor, but the theme of lost identity and its treatment belong to the generic *New Yorker* story, and the sign of the old man's displacement and alienation, the geranium, isn't a particularly happy choice. (O'Connor corrected these defects when she completely reworked the story in the last year of her life and published it under the title "Judgement Day.") "The Barber" is about a college teacher who gets caught in the snare of hatred while fighting racism. It owes much — too much — to Joyce's "A Little Cloud." "The Crop" seems to be an obligatory story for every young writer, an exorcism of sorts, in which the young author conjures up the image of herself as a failed writer and hopes to demonstrate in this way that she's immune to failure. O'Connor's hatchet job on her familiar, Miss Willerton, renders the character quite dead — before the story begins. "The Turkey" has a frankly spiritual theme. But the incident of the boy's capturing a wild turkey bears the weight of his spiritual musings only because they are trivial. When O'Connor steps in at the end with her vision of spirituality, the character is scared off, and the reader wishes O'Connor had been

writing at this deeper level from the beginning.

The best piece in the collection, "Wildcat," isn't a story but a sketch of two characters, an old black man who is blind and a young boy who shares his name, Gabriel. A wildcat has been out in the country, killing cattle, and the boy's heroic visions of hunting the cat and the fear the cat induces in the old man bring both characters to life. O'Connor maintains the dramatic tension throughout, and we find the sketch compelling even though it delivers only an encounter with two solid characters. That O'Connor could create the old black man, who is humorous without being a caricature, boded well.

"The Train" shows us that O'Connor has discovered the protagonist in *Wise Blood*, Hazel Motes (here called Hazel Wickers). In fact, O'Connor later rewrote this piece extensively

From 1945 to 1947 O'Connor attended the Writers Workshop, taught by Paul Engle. He was impressed by her quiet determination to become a better writer.

and used it as the opening segment of the novel. Not knowing Hazel well yet in "The Train," she depicts him as a mass of insecurity, not the prophet-despite-himself that he will become. She also doesn't know much of what he's up to, although she's detected that it has to do with the image of his dead mother's face as the casket lid closed on her. The last story O'Connor had finished in the collection, it shows that her prose style had gotten calamitously derailed by the influence of Thomas Wolfe. One sentence reads, "Now the train was greyflying past instants of trees and quick spaces of field and a motionless sky that sped darkening away in the opposite direction" (*CS,* p. 54).

O'Connor said later that if anyone would have told her how bad her early stories were, she would have stopped writing (*Letters,* p. 183). Her commentators can't help falling in love with her, and thus it seems they usually dismiss the statement as offhand. But I'm sure O'Connor was serious enough. It's not that the thesis stories don't show talent; it's simply that these stories are a quantum jump (more accurately in this case, a *leap*) away from being anything other than the stories of a graduate student — hundreds of such theses are filed away every year in never-to-be-opened archives. Flannery, on the far side of the leap, could look back and see the depth of the chasm. Her shudder shouldn't surprise us.

Flannery dedicated her thesis to Paul Engle. This man and the program he started were important enough to her that she stayed on an extra year after receiving her degree, working as a teaching assistant and laboring on her first novel. On the basis of her start on *Wise Blood* she was awarded the Rinehart-Iowa Prize for a first novel, which carried with it an option on the book. The fellowship must have encouraged her, but the option caused her difficulty later on.

*   *   *

Flannery spent most of 1948 at Yaddo, an artist's colony in Saratoga Springs, New York. Occupying five hundred acres of land, Yaddo has a central building, the Mansion, another large residence, West House, and outlying buildings hidden back in the woods that function as studios during the summer. Flannery stayed in West House during the winter, where she also had a study, and moved to the Mansion when she could be given a studio. A charitable institution, Yaddo enables its guests to carry on their artistic endeavors by providing them with work space and free room and board. The house rules seek to eliminate every distraction, including those a procrastinating artist might invent himself. Breakfast is served at a reasonably early hour, and then each artist is expected to hole up in his study or studio for the rest of the day. The delivery of box lunches helps insure that there will be no socializing until four o'clock. Everyone does gather for dinner and coffee afterwards. The Great Silence kept during working hours led one writer to describe Yaddo as a "swank monastery." Flannery found the strictures to her liking but the social life anything but monastic. In her correspondence she states frankly that a good deal of liquoring up and bedding down went on among the guests. Not prudish, she took this in stride and succeeded in making

friends without joining the bohemian frolics. "You survive in this atmosphere," she wrote, "by minding your own business and by having plenty of your own business to mind; and by not being afraid to be different from the rest of them" (*Letters*, p. 364).

Robert Lowell, Edward Maisel, and Elizabeth Hardwick were the other writers-in-residence during the winter after the first summer Flannery spent there. She became especially good friends with Lowell, calling him Cal as did his other friends.

The network of connections of the Yaddo community helped Flannery find a literary agent. Although she was still in the midst of writing *Wise Blood* and was, by her own reckoning, two years away from completing the project, she wrote to Elizabeth McKee on June 19, 1949, inquiring whether McKee would be interested in representing her work. By September Miss McKee had assented. The two women had a good working relationship for the entirety of Flannery's career.

Enthusiastic about her work, Lowell introduced Flannery to several of his literary friends on trips down to New York. Thus it was that Flannery met the publisher Robert Giroux, then at Harcourt, Brace, and a young poet and his wife, Robert and Sally Fitzgerald. The contact with Giroux turned out to be pivotal in Flannery's professional life, although neither had expected it to be. Because Flannery had received the Rinehart award, Rinehart held the option on her first novel. When Giroux and Flannery met in February of 1949, she had to inform him, to his disappointment, that her work was then committed elsewhere. But Rinehart had been given the first one-hundred-

Recent photographs of two of the people instrumental in O'Connor's career: Sally Fitzgerald (left) and Robert Giroux.

The Mansion at Yaddo, the artists' colony where O'Connor worked on Wise Blood.

eight pages of *Wise Blood* that previous fall, and the publisher had severe misgivings about the possible success of the novel. By the time of Flannery's winter meeting with Giroux, John Selby, the editor in charge of the project for Rinehart, had let Flannery know this; from his letter she drew the conclusion that he wanted "to train it [*Wise Blood*] into a conventional novel" (*Letters*, p. 9). She was not about to cooperate with his Procrustean plans, and she wrote to Elizabeth McKee on February 17, 1949, "I feel the objections they raise are connected with its virtues, and the thought of working with them specifically to correct these lacks they mention is repulsive to me" (*Letters*, p. 9). Timid in social situations, Flannery always knew what she was about as a writer, and while she was humble enough to act on helpful criticism, she never let anyone who did not have the perspicacity to appreciate her talent deflect her from her course.

Later, by October 1949, Rinehart gave up its option, releasing Flannery to find another publisher for the book. Having heard of the trouble between Flannery and Rinehart, Giroux had extended her a provisional contract that she could sign as soon as her relations with Rinehart were severed. Thus *Wise Blood* went from being under the care of one publisher to another without any anxious delay. The letter in which Rinehart declared that it would give up the option wasn't amicable, however, labeling Flannery "stiff-necked, uncooperative, and unethical" (*Letters*, p. 29). The memory of that letter irked Flannery for years afterward.

Troubling events eventually ushered Flannery out of Yaddo. Agnes Smedley, a journalist who was a Communist, had been at Yaddo for five years. Yaddo's purpose is to provide a respite from the pressures of earning a living, so the journalist's lengthy stay at Yaddo provoked suspicions, especially since she had published almost nothing during that time. Her activities attracted the attention of the FBI, and Yaddo was under surveillance during Smedley's final months there. Edward Maisel and Elizabeth Hardwick were questioned about the journalist. The four writers-in-residence wondered if the directress of the community wasn't guilty of letting Miss Smedley misuse the institution for her political purposes. Carefully the four prepared a statement of their apprehensions for the board of directors, agreeing to say nothing publicly until the board made its decision. Robert Lowell presented the questions and the evidence on which they were based. The board needed more information to make a final decision, but Lowell's presentation was plausible enough for the board to start a serious inquiry into the matter. Trying to protect the directress, one of the board members let influential people in the literary world read a transcript of the meeting. In the political climate then, with McCarthyism not far away, the four writers were publicly denounced for starting a witch-hunt. In protest they left Yaddo on March 1, 1949. Flannery's conservatism was reconfirmed by the unethical and public reprisals against the four's action. Lowell was devastated by having former friends turn against him. (See Sally Fitzgerald's interlinear editorial comments in *Letters*, pp. 11-12.) Flannery, provincial in most other respects to this Boston brahmin, knew the world to be a fallen place, and was not as surprised.

Flannery stayed in New York for about a month thereafter, finding an apartment on Broadway and 108th. She decamped to Milledgeville for a short visit, then returned to spend the summer. Her Barefoot-in-the-Park romance was brief. She found the city too much for her, enervating. She felt incapable of summoning the energy to brave her way down to the public library. Her forays into the outside world were largely restricted to eating in the Columbia University cafeteria — one of the few places she thought the food was clean — and to attending daily mass at a church on 107th Street.

Her friendship with the Fitzgeralds ripened during this time. Because they, like Flannery, were Catholics, she had much more in common with the young poet and his wife than with her other literary friends in New York. Soon the couple decided to move out to the country with their two children (Sally was expecting a third). They found a house with a room over the garage suited for a boarder; although Robert had a good teaching job at Sarah Lawrence, they needed rental income to help support the place. Hearing of their new home, Flannery volunteered to be their boarder, and she moved with them to Ridgefield, Connecticut, in September 1949.

Their life together quickly assumed its shape. Every day one of the parents drove with Flannery to Georgetown for morning mass while the other superintended breakfast with the children. The churchgoers would then return for breakfast, after which Flannery went back up to her room to work on *Wise Blood*. She emerged again about noon, taking her daily walk to the mailbox about a half-mile distant.

Every day she received a letter from Regina and mailed a reply. Apparently Flannery spent her afternoons reading, writing letters, and relaxing, having discovered that her morning stint of four hours was the maximum amount of time that she could devote to her fiction each day. After dinner, when the children had been put to bed, the Fitzgeralds and their boarder would have drinks and entertain themselves with good conversation. Having no plans to return to the South, Flannery's imagination was nevertheless alive with memories of Milledgeville, and invested itself in the current news Regina's letters brought. Although her mother still lived in town, she was running a dairy farm she had inherited called Andalusia. The name — which comes from a region of Spain known for its temperate climate — had been conferred by the penultimate owner before the farm passed into the hands of Regina's brother.

Christmas Day of 1950 was approaching when Flannery, typing up the first reading draft of *Wise Blood*, started to make jokes about her arms feeling heavy while she pecked away. She visited a doctor, who suspected rheumatoid arthritis; he advised her to have a thorough check-up at home during the Christmas holidays. On the train down to Milledgeville Flannery suffered her first attack of lupus. When she arrived she looked, her uncle remarked, "like a shriveled old woman." (See Sally Fitzgerald's editorial comments in *Letters*, pp. 21-22.)

The doctor who examined Flannery in Milledgeville at first accepted the tentative diagnosis of arthritis, then realized he needed another opinion. He consulted his friend in

Atlanta, Dr. Arthur J. Merrill. Over the phone Dr. Merrill correctly diagnosed Flannery's illness as lupus erythematosus. He asked that Flannery be brought into the city at once. As soon as Flannery was under his care, Dr. Merrill told Regina that Flannery's condition was serious and that she might die. Dr. Merrill, whom Flannery always referred to with affectionate sarcasm as "the scientist" in her letters, managed to save her life with blood transfusions and injections of the then-experimental drug, ACTH, a cortisone derivative. Flannery's high fevers finally passed, but then all her hair fell out and her faced swelled up, side effects of the ACTH. It became necessary to dehydrate her and put her on a salt-free diet.

Flannery was able to go home in the spring of 1951. Too weak to climb stairs, still on a salt-free diet, and giving herself injections of ACTH every day—which "send you off in a rocket," she told the Fitzgeralds (*Letters,* p. 26)—Flannery needed constant care and attention. Regina decided to move to Andalusia with Flannery and her Uncle Louis. At the farmhouse Flannery was given a suite of rooms on the first floor with access to the front porch. She regained her health slowly, with periodic stays in the hospital. Although there had been "nothing for it [lupus] but the undertaker" when her father had the disease, ACTH was able to control, though not cure, her condition (*Letters,* p. 57). Thus, afflicted with an "enduring chill," she took up residence at the place that was to be her home for the years remaining to her. She asked the Fitzgeralds to send down her books, all thoughts of carrying on the literary life in the North gone.

In the first full year of her illness she some-

how managed to complete revisions on *Wise Blood.* During this period she also made a valuable friend through correspondence. With Flannery's permission Robert Fitzgerald sent Caroline Gordon, the fiction writer and critic, a copy of the manuscript of *Wise Blood.* Gordon was a member of the agrarian movement at the start of her career, in which her husband, Allen Tate, played a prominent role, and she became increasingly interested in expressing a Christian vision. She saw at once what O'Connor was about as a writer in *Wise Blood.* Their common interests made the two women lasting friends. For the rest of her life O'Connor would send her stories and novels to Gordon for her critique, and she often benefitted greatly from the advice Gordon offered on her work in progress. For example, O'Connor would expand the middle section of *The Violent Bear It Away* at the prompting of Gordon and others in order to bring out Rayber's character.

From 1952 to 1955 Flannery was most productive by any standards, completing the short stories in her first published collection, *A Good Man Is Hard to Find.* As ACTH proved reliable, her anxieties were no doubt gradually allayed. She was absorbed in her work and the growing flock of peafowl she introduced to Andalusia. She seems to have accepted the restrictions of her life with surprising alacrity. Her major concern was always for her work, and once she saw that her life at Andalusia would not hinder it—saw that living in the South would, in fact, enhance her work, something she must have realized in writing the collection of stories—she gained a sense, albeit a reluctant one, that she was being blessed by this deprivation. In 1955 ACTH was replaced

The ravages of lupus: O'Connor in 1952 at age 27.

by Merticorten, a medication that Flannery was able to take orally (she had to take ACTH by injection) and that eliminated the necessity of a salt-free diet. This allowed her to become more comfortable with her illness.

Until she developed the fibroid tumor that precipitated her final struggle with lupus, Flannery remained in fair health. She did, however, experience a deterioration of her leg and hip bones (later her jaw was similarly affected), which necessitated that she walk on crutches. Her description of her need of crutches is typical of her outward attitude toward her illness. "I will henceforth," she wrote, "be a structure with flying buttresses" (*Letters*, p. 151). She was always joking, hiding the pain. The good humor in her letters strikes us sometimes as horribly sad. We may feel that she should have expressed her natural anger and resentment of her condition, if only to let others comfort her as best they could. But a crucial distinction applies here. Although Flannery suppressed her anguish, she did not repress it. The depth of that suffering would emerge later, but only after she had waited until she could see its extension of meaning. "I have never been anywhere but sick," she wrote to a friend. "In a sense sickness is a place, more instructive than a long trip to Europe, and it's always a place where there's no company, where nobody can follow. Sickness before death is a very appropriate thing and I think those who don't have it miss one of God's mercies" (*Letters*, p. 163).

Scenes of present-day Milledgeville. O'Connor was frequently labeled a small-town Southern writer, a false tag she often parodied. In one letter to her good friend Maryat Lee, she began, "Greetings from historic Milledgeville where the ladies and gents wash in separate tubs. . . . My standard is: when in Rome, do as you done in Milledgeville."

Wise Blood

WHEN *Wise Blood* was published in 1952, Flannery's neighbors celebrated the event, staging a number of functions in her honor. The biggest, a tea, had the telephone book as the source of the guest list. Few in Milledgeville understood *Wise Blood* — few people in the world did at first — and some were shocked by the language Mary Flannery had used. Most remained polite, however, and Flannery returned the favor, concealing her wounded scorn as best she could. Her relatives treated the matter as a family concern, and were more free with their opinions. One ancient cousin wrote to say, "I do not like your book" (*Letters*, p. 138). But they in no way rejected Flannery herself, and she was glad they could dispense with the book without losing their love for her. The critics generally misread the novel, mistaking the grotesque for the comic and the comic for the grotesque.

As in many modern and contemporary novels, not much seems to happen in *Wise Blood*. The actions that do take place may seem to occur without warning and fade away without consequences. Appearances could not be more deceiving. Having been discharged from the army, the protagonist, Hazel Motes, has returned to his hometown — Eastrod, Tennessee — to find it deserted, his family's home dilapidated and abandoned. He sets off for the city, Taulkinham, to become a free-lance evangelist like the deceased grandfather he closely resembles. His grandfather had had Jesus "hidden in his head like a stinger" (*WB*, p. 120), but the gospel Hazel preaches is unbelief, and the church to which he calls disciples must be the Church Without Christ. His mission brings him into contact with a freakish assortment of people, all of whom gradually lose touch with him; finally, self-blinded, he stumbles away from the last of them to die.

In *Wise Blood* O'Connor won her way through to the narrative method that characterizes her mature work. A later story, "Good Country People," includes a passage in which the main character, Hulga, dreams of duping a Bible salesman, and the tactics she thinks of using are patterned after those O'Connor employs:

> She was to meet the Bible salesman at ten o'clock at the gate. She had thought about it half the night. She had started thinking of it as a great joke and then she had begun to see profound implications in it. She had lain in bed imagining dialogues for them that were insane on the surface but that reached below to depths that no Bible salesman would be aware of. (*CS*, pp. 282-83)

Wise Blood struck the critics as a fiendishly extended exercise in the use of irony, a "great joke." A close reading — with the advantage of O'Connor's entire corpus, her essays, and her letters before us — reveals implications that

The Roman Catholic church that O'Connor attended in Milledgeville. She thought that faith was a gift — but a challenging one: "What people don't realize is how much religion costs. They think faith is a big electric blanket, when of course it is the cross. It is much harder to believe than not to believe."

O'Connor at the autographing party for Wise Blood *held at Georgia College in Milledgeville (1952).*

underwent revision after revision, with scores of episodes finally discarded and a host of characters compressed into its final troupe. O'Connor did, however, shape and finish the book according to her original intention: to present the dramatic and logical consequences of a pilgrimage through sin.

In an early summary of the book that she prepared for the benefit of possible publishers, she wrote, "All he [Hazel Motes] has retained of the evangelical religion of his mother is a sense of sin. . . . This sense of sin is the only key he has to finding a sanctuary and he begins unconsciously to search for God through sin." *Wise Blood* might have been entitled *The Terrain of Sin* or *The Wasteland Revisited.* In it O'Connor maps out a world inhabited by characters who so personify dimensions of evil that they threaten to rise off the ground of being into an allegorical sky. In several instances they remain in contact with the earth only on tiptoe, like figures in the flat space of medieval paintings. These "dimensions" might be better thought of — to correct the extended metaphor — as demons. Hazel Motes comes among them as another Legion, assailed by all the evil spirits as he goes backward toward Bethlehem (cf. *Wise Blood*, p. 219).

Haze begins by trying what we might think of as good, old-fashioned sin. He's determined to rid himself of the "wild ragged figure" of Jesus, who moves "from tree to tree in the back of his mind . . . motioning him to turn around and come off into the dark where he was not sure of his footing, where he might be walking on the water and not know it and then suddenly know it and drown" (*WB*, p. 22). Trying to direct his attention away from this

proceed from modern life as it is lived into intellectual history, implications that we would have thought remote at first. Insane on the surface, *Wise Blood* drives us toward the truth and the sanity its discovery brings with it.

O'Connor, finding herself "possessed of the modern consciousness, that thing Jung describes as unhistorical, solitary, and guilty," understood that modern man's last tenuous contact with the supernatural came through the bond of sin and guilt. After being weakened by a psychological critique, that bond had been given new strength by the horrors of the age: the Holocaust, the bomb, et cetera. Strands (like sexual mores) that had frayed were replaced with new ties: absurdity, angst, and a flattening of emotion that came with the breaking of old taboos. *Wise Blood* took O'Connor five years to write, and its action haunting obsession, he moves in with Leora Watts, a prostitute, when he arrives in the city. Since he has remained chaste through his army years, he expects his newfound carnal knowledge to bring with it profound changes in his life. But the experience leaves him feeling nothing more than embarrassment—he performs badly the first time and has to steel himself for his next amorous night with Leora, who is a tub of flesh. He ends up staying with her for as long as he does "not for the sake of the pleasure in her, but to prove that he didn't believe in sin since he practiced what was called it" (*WB*, p. 110).

His next paramour turns out to be Sabbath Lily Hawks. Sabbath lives in a boardinghouse with her father, Asa, a preacher who failed in his attempt to blind himself with quicklime "to justify his belief that Christ had redeemed him" (*WB*, p. 112). From that day, however, Asa has acted the part of the blind preacher, using the ruse of his handicap to attract crowds and bamboozle them. Believing Asa's blindness to be real and his faith to be in earnest, Haze decides to seduce his daughter, and in despoiling an innocent girl justify his belief that virtue has no claim upon him. With this act he will progress from "plain sin" to sacrilege, a premeditated profanation of the sacred. He hopes to bring the preacher to despair as well and thus efface what he presumes to be the condemning reality of the man's faith. But Sabbath turns out to be far from innocent: she's more than equally intent on seducing Haze. She tells him that when she first saw him, she said to herself, "Look at those pee-can eyes and go crazy, girl! That innocent look don't hide a thing, he's just pure filthy right

down to the guts, like me. The only difference is I like being that way and he don't" (*WB*, p. 169).

O'Connor wryly alludes to Nathanael West's *Miss Lonelyhearts* by having Sabbath initiate her seduction by referring to the letters she sent to Mary Brittle, an advice-to-the-lovelorn columnist. She tells Haze that she wrote and asked—since she is a bastard and bastards are not allowed to enter the kingdom of heaven anyway—whether it might be all right for her to enjoy herself in the here and now by necking. Mary Brittle advised her to examine her religious beliefs in the light of modern mores and read some books on ethical culture. Sabbath saw the columnist had missed her point; she was adjusted to the modern world all right, but would it be right for her to go all the way? O'Connor at once makes Sabbath's seduction of Haze perfectly roundabout, as a fifteen-year-old girl would do it, and acknowledges her debt to and her differences with West. The *Miss Lonelyhearts* columnist presumes his innocence and that of his correspondents; their mutual problems derive from a lack of knowledge. O'Connor follows Saint Paul in his teaching that natural revelation, the book of this world read by our conscience, declares God's holiness and our own depravity. For West, the problem is what we know or can't know; for O'Connor, the problem is who we are.

Haze tries desperately to deny sin, but Sabbath's triumph and his dealings with the book's other characters only serve to verify the reality of sin for him. The satanic logic of his rebellion breaks down because it is a counterfeit version of the truth, as Satan is God's counterfeit. Christ redeemed a sinful world by living a sinless life and dying not for his sins but ours. Haze tries to redeem a sinless world by living a sinful life; he attempts to sacrifice his own innocence in order to wipe out the distinction between good and evil. But he keeps being brought up short by the world's corruption—his naiveté is essential. And yet at the moment he discovers a new twist to evil, he also discovers it within himself in inchoate form; it's there anterior to any discrete act. Original sin, pride in all its manifestations, keeps disqualifying him as a savior—he's "pure filthy." In one scene he tells the blind preacher, "If I was in sin I was in it before I ever committed any" (*WB*, p. 53). That's the truth, but he resists it. As a boy, we are to remember, he tromped through the woods in rock-filled shoes to keep the books balanced, to avoid having to believe in the atonement. When his mother admonished him that Jesus died to redeem him, he replied, "I never ast him" (*WB*, p. 63). Since then he has seen that he cannot avoid Jesus by avoiding sin—he has lost his footing on his seven-story mountain of purgatory—and therefore he continues his descent purposefully, trying to get to the bottom of sin. Hell is a bottomless pit, however. His every effort to redeem the world from redemption simply heightens his awareness that either sin needs redeeming or its absurdity is intolerable.

Few can live with this tension. Haze preaches that his Church Without Christ is "the church that the blood of Jesus don't foul with redemption" (*WB*, p. 105). The small crowds he attracts turn away. Like Haze, they do not want to admit their own depravity, but unlike him, they insist on palliative forms of belief. Their bad faith finds expression in the one disciple Haze does attract, Hoover Shoats, who has worked as a radio preacher under the name Onnie Jay Holy. O'Connor uses him to parody the false forms of religion that appeal to this weakness. They all, O'Connor seems to be saying, begin with the Romantic demythologizing whereby everyone's childhood replaces Eden as our age of innocence. When Onnie Jay comes on the scene, he scores an immediate hit with the crowd. He jumps up on the hood of Haze's car and declares,

> "Every person that comes onto this earth . . . is born sweet and full of love. A little child loves ever'body, friends, and its nature is sweetness—until something happens. Something happens, friends, I don't need to tell people like you that can think for theirselves. As this little child gets bigger, its sweetness don't show so much, cares and troubles come to perplext it, and all its sweetness is driven inside it. Then it gets miserable and lonesome and sick, friends. It says, 'Where is all my sweetness gone? where are all the friends that loved me?' and all the time, that little beat-up rose of its sweetness is inside, not a petal dropped, and on the outside is just a mean lonesomeness." (*WB*, pp. 150-51)

Haze scorns Onnie Jay Holy and his gospel of the lake district. Onnie Jay renames Haze's Church Without Christ the Holy Church of Christ Without Christ, doubling the absurdity but making it far more palatable to the crowd who can "think for theirselves." In Onnie Jay we confront not so much sin itself but the effect of sin, how in rationalizing it we kill the truth that would make us free. The dust from a thousand dead ideologies whips across the reaches of this wasteland. After sin's first pleasures, we experience its deathliness, the cauterizing of affection and love, and the lostness of placing our trust in guides that cannot lead us to our true country.

That a capable huckster like Onnie Jay latches onto Haze strikes us as unlikely until he explains that he believes Haze has "good idears," but what he needs is "an artist-type" to work with (*WB*, p. 157). He's responding to Haze's call for a "new jesus." Apparently he believes that Haze has this new jesus stashed away, and he offers his friendship in order to steal the new jesus for his own evangelistic sideshow.

Haze uses the figure of a new jesus, as Nietzsche used Zarathustra, to proclaim a darkly Romantic gospel of heroic rebellion in the face of absurdity: an ethic of might makes right, with the victims of the strong somehow happy to have let the dominant step all over them. The new jesus is a way "to say a thing," to praise man's ability to shake his fist in the face of a god who isn't there. But another character, Enoch Emery, also takes Haze's call for a new jesus literally, and in so doing moves the action of the novel onto a different plane.

Enoch is an eighteen-year-old boy who has been abandoned by his father and now works at the city park, guarding an entrance. He is the character who introduces the notion of "wise blood." He feels compulsions that lead him to behave in ways that are so mysterious that he can't even question them. "Enoch's brain," we are told, "was divided into two parts. The part in communication with his blood did the figuring but it never said anything in words.

The other part was stocked up with all kinds of words and phrases" (*WB*, p. 87). Enoch is a wonderful comic character and provides some of the best scenes and lines in the book. We can't forget his hiding in the bushes close to a public swimming pool in order to view the somewhat slack figure of a young mother sunning herself in a bathing suit — and here's the naughty bit — that has a decorative split at each hip. But, as always with O'Connor, we need to remember that the maximum amount of comedy admits the maximum amount of seriousness. Enoch is a primitive, but that's not to say that his is a simple case or that what's primitive about him is unfortunate. He believes he has "wise blood." Ah, how pathetically wrong such souls can be, we may at first think. But then we see that Enoch does indeed have wise blood. His problem, to be grand about it, is a dissociation of sensibility taken to the nth degree, the cleavage between that part of his brain in communication with his blood and the higher centers of thought that house nothing but stock phrases. This half-wit represents the majority of us, and not only the worst in us but something of the best as well.

In many ways Enoch has a greater natural capacity for religious experience than anyone else in the novel, including Haze. Possessing an innate sense of liturgy, he invests his life with meaning through repeated actions that gradually assume the character of a rite. Every day at quitting time he leaves his post at the park entrance to encounter the mystery that is at the heart of the park. First he visits the Frosty Bottle, a hotdog stand in the shape of an Orange Crush, to have a sacramental milkshake. (We can't dispute its sacred character because when he takes Haze along to visit the mystery, he insists on enacting this ritual — and the other actions of his liturgy — even though he runs the risk of losing his companion, whom he wants desperately as a friend and co-religionist.) Next he goes to the zoo and passes by cages of bears and monkeys. Preparing for a direct encounter with the mystery, he must warm up by confronting these powers and principalities. The long corridor of the animal cages suggests ritual purification through undergoing a trial, running a gauntlet. He despises the animals, lingering at one cage one time, another cage the next, to insult and spit upon them. But we should not think of this experience exclusively in terms of descent, a harrowing. Enoch envies the animals' state, their lolling about in company (he's excruciatingly lonely) and their diet — T-bone steaks delivered regularly by their servants, the zoo employees. Through encountering these august presences, therefore, he also rises, ascends, into a state of blessing that prepares him for the mystery. Finally he enters the holy of holies, the tabernacle of his god, a museum of natural history. The very word *museum* summons up feelings of awe — the letter *u* in *museum* is patterned after Roman lettering and thus appears as a *v*, and the vibrations of *musevm* are almost as unspeakable to Enoch as the tetragrammaton. After entering the building, he confronts the mystery directly, visiting a room that houses, in a "coffin-like" case, a shrunken man, a mummy that has been reduced to the size of an infant. In all of this there are refractions of sacramentalism and also a more direct form of communion with God — mystic union — for Enoch leaves behind the medium

of his milkshake and the animals to be in virtual contact with his deity. When Haze calls for a new jesus, Enoch knows where to find him.

Enoch steals the mummy out of the case and takes it to his apartment. The Christian imagery builds in this segment: Enoch paints the inside of his washstand's cabinet with gilt, preparing a tabernacle for the reserved sacrament he will later present to Haze. Enoch himself anticipates that the theft will accomplish a great change in his life. Shortly after the deed is done, he tells a waitress in a diner that something's going to happen to him: "You may not see me again . . . the way I am" (*WB*, p. 194). Clearly, Enoch believes he's about to be saved — from his loneliness, isolation, and meager endowment of natural gifts — by this single action for which, he thinks, the entire course of his life has been preparing him.

After Enoch delivers his sacred package, Haze, who has earlier been taken by Enoch to visit the mummy, recognizes that he has indeed been presented with a new jesus — a jesus shrunken to the size to which Hazel's unbelief would tailor him; a jesus that is a continuing sign of our mortality, that lives on in a mummified eternity only to proclaim the impossibility of resurrection. The mummy's eyes "were drawn almost shut as if a giant block of steel were falling down on top of him" (*WB*, p. 98). The weight of time is too much for the merely mortal to bear. Haze throws the mummy out a door that once led to a fire escape (a nice image for Protestantism) but now opens upon nothing.

Enoch, however, is rewarded by his god. He seizes the chance to steal a gorilla costume from a man who's being taken around the city to promote a new movie about its eponymous star, Gonga. Enoch believes he will impress others in the gorilla suit, as he was impressed earlier when he saw Gonga in front of a movie theater. Pathetically, he was moved then to confess his loneliness to this figure, who had extended what seemed a friendly hand. But after a moment the promotional ape-man interrupted him and told him to go to hell. After Enoch dons the suit, his ceremonial gesture of extending his hand to a pair of lovers fails just as miserably. The frightened couple swiftly retreats. Still, at the moment of metamorphosis, "no gorilla in existence, whether in the jungles of Africa or California, or in New York City in the finest apartment in the world, was happier at that moment than this one, whose god had finally rewarded it" (*WB*, pp. 197-98).

At this point Enoch lifts toward allegory; O'Connor didn't want us to miss her critique of our misdirected religious impulses. Enoch is not the only one with two minds: all of us suffer from this division of faith and reason. Our religious impulses, we have to admit, are often misdirected toward the mummified idols of apartments in the Dakota, BMWs, and hot tubs. By capitulating to our instinctive drives and felt needs—we don't think about moral standards anymore; we simply assume anything is all right as long as it doesn't hurt anyone else—we have been rewarded by the loss of our humanity. Enoch is actually better off than most; he has his loneliness in the end to tell him he's been wrong. Most of us are too busy pursuing our idols to notice the emptiness inside our designer gorilla suits.

Asa Hawks, the street-corner evangelist,

at first appears to be nothing more than a mountebank, the source of his daughter's hypocrisy and an aid—until he's dispatched to the high seas on a banana boat (a paradise of food for another gorilla?)—to the novel's action. We are glad when Haze steals into his room and with the lighting of one match discovers that Asa's blindness is a sham. We are ready to dispense with him at this point. Yet Asa prefigures Haze's fate; he plays a role that Haze will enact. In the other characters we have examined, Haze has discovered a sinful form of escape from his obsession with God, and one by one he has found them ineffective or repulsive. But after discovering Asa's secret, Haze feels free of the constraints of authentic belief only for a time. When he isn't merely begging, Asa himself continues to be almost at the mercy of an action—his self-blinding—that he didn't carry off. The other characters are buried within their selves; their characters are one with their behavior. Asa, however, shares with Haze an ambivalence that leads both to play self-created roles—Asa one of belief, Haze one of unbelief. In Asa, Haze meets a soul that, like his, is divided against itself. There is enough of the believer in Asa that he continues to disturb the unbeliever in Haze until Haze makes his desperate peace with that image. In this connection we might note that Haze hardly has a normal conversation with anyone; time after time he answers the pleasantries of others with nonsequiturs about redemption that, through their repetition, beg us to fill in the arguments for the other side. It's like listening to someone on the telephone. With Asa, however, Haze resorts to evasive pleasantries because he recognizes him as someone capable of arguing the other side. Haze sees in Asa a mirror image with the symmetrical halves of belief and unbelief reversed. Asa is an alter ego, a kind of double — or, to use the term of O'Connor's beloved Conrad, a "secret sharer."

Asa and Hazel's reaction to him help us understand the central metaphor in *Wise Blood*: blindness. The way in which O'Connor uses blindness is indeed a key to how her imagination works throughout the body of her mature work. She takes the metaphoric dimensions of blindness as they are found in the Bible and pushes them as far as possible toward the literal. She begins with having Asa pronounce the words of Christ to Haze as a diagnosis of his condition. "You got eyes and see not, ears and hear not," he says, then adds a prophetic forecast — "but you'll have to see sometime" (*WB*, p. 54). She expands these comments and reinforces their meaning through other observations Asa makes. From their first encounter on a street corner, where a salesman delivers his spiel for a potato peeler, Asa recognizes the "urge for Jesus" in Haze's voice. " 'Some preacher has left his mark on you,' the blind man said with a kind of snicker. 'Did you follow for me to take it off or give you another one?' " (*WB*, p. 51). Asa is right, of course, on all counts. Haze's grandfather has left his mark on Haze — Haze looks like him — and we hear the need for Jesus, as Asa does, in his protestations. We may think that O'Connor is simply using Asa, playing with the irony of placing the truth on the tongue of a false prophet. She certainly uses Enoch's lack of wits to present before Haze the dessicated horror of his call for a new jesus. But Asa, unlike any other character in the book, save

at the last for Haze, has had a real encounter with the holy. We are meant to read this early episode in the light of the decisive moment when Asa took up the quicklime.

The article that Asa shows Haze about his blindness reads, "Asa Hawks, an evangelist of the Free Church of Christ, has promised to blind himself to justify his belief that Christ had redeemed him" (*WB*, p. 112). Here "justify" means to prove or vindicate. If Asa is willing to give up his sight, the logic of the incident runs, then his belief in Christ must be in earnest. The act would then have been something like a herculean trial — like Enoch's filing past the animal cages — a task that must be accomplished to earn the blessing of his god. But, unlike Hercules, the God to whom Asa has been testifying has not asked this of him; only the god-of-hoodwinked-followers desires it. Thus the incident stands as a demonic stunt, a trick of a demagogue who has finally succumbed to his own lies. At the crucial moment Christ makes this clear, taking away Asa's will to let the quicklime seep into his eyes:

> He had been possessed of as many *devils* as were necessary to do it, but at that instant, they disappeared, and he saw himself standing there as he was. He fancied *Jesus, Who had expelled them,* was standing there too, beckoning to him; and he had fled out of the tent into the alley and disappeared. (*WB*, p. 114, italics mine)

Asa is a failure as an evangelist not because he failed to take his own sight but because he ran away from his one real encounter with the holy. He could have turned to God, we may speculate, and confessed his error to the people; instead, fearing the true sacrifice that holiness entails — usually an agony of the mundane — he retreats into a life of selfish isolation. The only remaining signs of his encounter with God are his ability to recognize a desire for God in others and, paradoxically, his ruse of blindness. This sham carries a double and painful irony; it shows forth the two prongs of his hopelessness. For in the sense of Christ's words, he is self-blinded, willfully opposed to his own redemption, the possibility of which he ironically justified when for a moment he was given the eyes to see.

O'Connor uses another secret sharer, Solace Layfield, to precipitate Haze's final crisis of unbelief, bringing his quest through sin to its logical conclusion. Hoover Shoats reappears in front of those cathedrals of secularism, movie theaters, to call people into the Holy Church of Christ Without Christ. Since Haze has shown himself to be intractable, Hoover has found his own new jesus: the True Prophet, Solace, whom he dresses in a glare-blue suit and white hat identical to those Haze wears. We are told little about Solace himself, only that he is a consumptive with six children and that playing the True Prophet is about as hard as he wants to work. The similarity of Solace and Haze in dress and even in look — especially in the absence of information that would give the character of Solace a certain weight — begs us to identify the author's symbolic intentions. Here again the narrative tends to rise away from naturalism. Standing among the crowd that Hoover and the True Prophet have drawn the first night, Haze bumps elbows with a woman who asks, "Him [the True Prophet]

and you twins?" Haze replies enigmatically, "If you don't hunt it down and kill it, it'll hunt you down and kill you." The only gloss on what Haze means comes when the woman turns to another person in the crowd and comments, "He's nuts. . . . I never seen no twins that hunted each other down" (*WB*, p. 168).

But we are about to see Haze do just that. To understand his violent hatred of his double, the associations of these comments must be strung together like the metaphors of a poem. Throughout the novel Haze seems to be carrying on an inner dialogue that issues forth in nonsequiturs in his conversation. For a time Asa Hawks substitutes for the other side of Haze that the nihilist in him wants to shout down. The appearance of Solace, with "the resemblance in their clothes and possibly in their faces" (*WB*, p. 202), must seem to Haze an apparition of his other self, particularly because Solace preaches on the one thing that Haze at all costs does not want to admit to himself: his need for and thus his virtual belief in Jesus. The twins of belief and unbelief have been "hunting each other down" from the first page of *Wise Blood*. The verb "hunt" reminds us of the hound of heaven, of course, and in this context, of that ragged figure. Ironically, Solace really is for us a "true prophet," because he stands for what Haze would be if he were united with that figure.

In his quest to rid himself of Jesus, Haze has traveled through straightforward sin (in fornication) and through blasphemy (in his deflowering of Sabbath) and the Romanticism of being his own jesus, a heroic rebel against the absurdity of life. Sin turned out to be embarrassing; blasphemy taught him that "you couldn't even believe in that because then you were believing in something to blaspheme" (*WB*, p. 206). And now his dark Romanticism compels him to perform one last desperate act of transvaluing all values, an act not sacrificial in its character, as was the oblation of his chastity, but aggressive, an exercise of power in the service of self-transcendence. After that evening's street-corner service, Haze tails Solace (an openly allegorical name) when he drives home, rams his double's car off the road, and then, because he so desperately wants to believe that Solace "ain't true" (*WB*, p. 204) — that his own belief that he is projecting onto this woebegone fellow doesn't exist — runs over Solace with his car and kills him. Standing next to him after this violent act, Haze hears Solace's dying words, "Jesus hep me" (*WB*, p. 205). This last-minute confession mocks Haze's efforts and shows them to be in vain. We sense that if Haze silenced every believing voice in the world, the stones would cry out against him.

Haze succeeds in murdering Solace, but he fails to accomplish his real intention: the self-murder of *his* solace, his believing self. In this episode O'Connor shows us that a search through sin, the ordinary path of liberation in our time, while it promises freedom and an increased vitality, finally ends up being masochistic and suicidal. We *are* made in the image of God, and those who are honest with themselves, as Haze is, will find it impossible, short of suicide, to quell that self that insists upon its supernatural character. However hard he tries, Haze cannot escape the sacrificial character of life nor accomplish the sacrifice that will redeem him from redemption. His integ-

rity, as O'Connor herself suggests in her preface to the second edition of the novel, consists in what he cannot do: slay the part of him that sees that ragged figure.

Haze's Nietzschean Romanticism quickly gives way to a brief infection of logical positivism. About to leave for another city, Haze explains to a young gas-station attendant that "it was not right to believe anything you couldn't see or hold in your hands or test with your teeth" (*WB*, p. 206). Although he slams the boy's water bucket on the concrete to emphasize what he's saying, he doesn't believe it for a moment. Nihilism is in the air Haze breathes, so he tries to be "the stinkingest logical positivist you ever saw." But his underlying belief, the last to be jettisoned before his quest turns penitent, finds its object in that distinctively American idol: the automobile. "He said nobody with a good car needed to worry about anything" (*WB*, p. 206). But shortly after Haze sets out for that next city, that paradise that has always receded farther west as Americans have gone after it, a sheriff stops him and pushes his old wreck off the road. Even before the literal destruction of the car, however, Haze "had the sense that the road was really slipping back under him. He had known all along that there was no more country but he didn't know that there was not another city" (*WB*, p. 207). The world is either part of the kingdom of God or part of the devil's terrain; every city is either Jerusalem or Babylon.

So Hazel Motes undertakes the literal fulfillment of a commandment lodged in his very name. Jesus admonished his followers to cast out the beam that was in their own eye before they tried to remove the mote, the speck of dust, in another's eye. For, as he asked, can the blind lead the blind? (cf. Luke 6:39-42). The splinter obscuring Haze's vision is the entire twentieth century. "If thine eye be evil," Jesus also said, "thy whole body shall be full of darkness. If therefore the light that is in thee be darkness, how great *is* that darkness!" (Matt. 6:23). Haze's soul is immersed in an ocean of darkness, where he — fathoms deep, like those fish that live in the eternal night of the depths — must supply his own light with the small phosphorescent generator of sin. That is why O'Connor has Haze literally carry out Christ's hyperbolic instruction: "If thine eye offend thee, pluck it out" (Matt. 18:9). For she could not have taken the last half of that verse more seriously: "it is better for thee to enter into life [the kingdom of God] with one eye, rather than having two eyes to be cast into hell fire."

How can Christ call Haze to blind himself when he appears to Asa — as Jehovah did to Abraham when he lifted the knife above Isaac — in order to stay his hand? O'Connor lets secondary questions about the propriety of Haze's self-blinding and his ensuing ascetical practices stand moot; primarily, she wants to show us the reality of what is at stake — heaven and hell — as starkly as Christ did in his use of hyperbole. We must see, however, that the fundamental distinction between asceticism and simple masochism applies. Legitimate ascetical practices are never an end in themselves; they are to be countenanced only as a means toward a deeper communion with God. Asa was trying to attract attention to himself; Haze blinds himself to distractions from God. One act is self-serving; the other

places its agent in the position of a servant. Still, the violence of Haze's self-blinding, the walks he begins to take thereafter in shoes filled with gravel, stones, and broken glass, and the barbed wire he wears as a kind of hair shirt may seem of a piece with his murder of Solace Layfield. Part of the difficulty arises from our tendency to associate divine charity with what's nice. God's war against Satan, we must remember, is also a part of his charity — a point O'Connor makes again in her second novel, *The Violent Bear It Away* (the title of which is taken from Matt. 11:12: "The kingdom of heaven suffereth violence and the violent bear it away"). Paradoxically, the murder and Haze's ascetical practices are polar opposites. The impulse of the murder is essentially suicidal; sin results not in liberation but in self-destruction: it's life-denying. Asceticism, on the other hand, affirms life. As fallen creatures we participate in Christ's redemption of the world and his restoration of our own souls by offering up our sin to Christ, by letting it be put to death in his person on the cross. What most people misunderstand is that asceticism should not be a means to further self-abasement; rather, it should help us *discover* the extent to which we are already fallen. It provides insights that lead to penitence; in the humility of remorse we are then enabled to respond to and make efficacious Christ's sacrifice.

Another aspect of suffering often gets mixed up in and corrupts asceticism as a process of discovery. The church also teaches that we may offer up our own suffering — the diminishments that come to us because Satan holds this world captive, that burden us through no fault of our own — and make them part of, an enlargement of, Christ's own innocent suffering. The key here is that we cannot be responsible for the pain through which we identify with Christ's passion and in a mysterious way are allowed to add to it. Haze does make this mistake; he gets the two mixed up, as many religious have in church history. He goes to unwarranted lengths, makes uncalled-for sacrifices, that cause his death. This partially obscures the antinomies at work: redemption and sin, asceticism and suicide, penance and suffering, life and death.

Yet there can be no doubt that heaven honors Haze's attempt to "get clean"—if unadulterated virtue were required of our strivings toward God, they would all be in vain. (Protestants, of course, press this very point and conclude that our salvation must be attributable to grace alone. But they, too, recognize that God works through our acts in the process they would prefer to call sanctification rather than redemption.) The mystery of holiness is so difficult to express directly, however, that O'Connor resorts to an ingenious cloaking technique in the figure of Mrs. Flood, Haze's landlady. The course of Mrs. Flood's relationship with her boarder recapitulates the ground Haze has already covered, and allows us to know, to witness, Haze's journey into the mystery of holiness—not directly but through its effect on Mrs. Flood. Fiction must always be an incarnational art, and as such it must work completely by analogy, through outward signs of the inward. Haze therefore stands in relation to Mrs. Flood as Christ stands in relation to us: he is a mediator of the divine for her, as Christ is the mediator between us and the Father.

Mrs. Flood is virtually an allegorical figure who represents the flood of secularism; we would be hard-pressed to discover an aspect of it she doesn't embody. Outwardly the most normal person in the book, she is in all truth the most grotesque inhabitant of this wasteland. Her capacity for awe and wonder and even pleasure is almost nil. "She had had a hard life, without pain and without pleasure" (*WB*, p. 229). Mrs. Flood might be Eliot's typist ("Well, that's done [her seduction], and I'm glad it's over"), aged thirty years and set down in Macon, Georgia. Her one avenue to the sacred comes through sin: she is greedy. We are told that she cannot look at anything for long without wanting it. This attracts her to Haze and to what he may have found in his darkness. She begins to stare "into his face as if she expected to see something she hadn't seen before. This irritated her with him and gave her the sense that he was cheating her in some secret way" (*WB*, p. 213). In his presence she begins to suspect that there's something valuable that she doesn't see, something "hidden near her but out of her reach" (*WB*, p. 222). When she finds out that the army pays Hazel a pension and that he simply throws away any extra money at the end of the week, she plans to marry him, have him committed, and become the beneficiary of his pension. Concluding, however, that there must be some reason for his odd behavior—for she cannot conceive of anybody doing anything for any motive other than self-interest—she comes to see that the darkness in which he lives is the treasure he possesses. Her avarice leads her to desire to penetrate that darkness and "see for herself what was there" (*WB*, p. 225). In the absence of any explanation other than cryptic statements from Haze like "If there's no bottom in your eyes, they hold more" (*WB*, p. 222), the landlady is forced to imagine what that darkness must be like:

> She thought of her own head as a switchbox where she controlled from; but with him, she could only imagine the outside in, the whole black world in his head and his head bigger than the world, his head big enough to include the sky and planets and whatever was or had been or would be. How would he know if time was going backwards or forwards or if he was going with it? She imagined it was like you were walking in a tunnel and all you could see was a pin point of light. She had to imagine the pin point of light; she couldn't think of it at all without that. She saw it as some kind of a star, like the star on Christmas cards. She saw him going backwards to Bethlehem and she had to laugh. (*WB*, pp. 218-19)

So this woman, who has lived without pleasure or pain, who seemingly has never had an unconventional thought in her life, comes to perceive at least a pin point of light, of revelation — which is an Eliotian still point, an intersection of the timeless with time — through the prophetic faculty of the imagination. After Haze's death, the landlady "sat staring with her eyes shut, into his eyes, and felt as if she had finally got to the beginning of something she couldn't begin, and she saw him moving farther and farther away, farther and farther into the darkness until he was the pin point of light" (*WB*, p. 232). Thus Haze has performed the miracle of awakening Mrs. Flood's once-dormant religious sensibilities, and he has led her, and us, to the entrance of eternity. Here we, like Augustine in the garden outside Milan, must wait for the grace to will what we know to be true. In this wasteland the rose may yet bloom once again.

Five years in its composition, *Wise Blood* was that quantum leap into maturity for which O'Connor had been actively waiting. During those five years she not only found the final shape of *Wise Blood* in what must have seemed a never-ending process of revision; she also found the true country of her imagination, the kind of fiction she could make come to life. In this novel we witness the birth of *the* O'Connor. She will mature further, of course, but her imaginative endowment, her peculiar genius, has now been vouchsafed. The gem of her vocation has been cut, revealing the brilliance of its structure.

"The Displaced Person"

O'Connor in 1953. She never looked comfortable in photographs, and in fact she wasn't. After having her picture taken for the jacket of Wise Blood, *she sent this stinging report to Robert and Sally Fitzgerald: "I had to go have my picture taken for the purposes of Harcourt, Brace. They were all bad. (The pictures.) The one I sent looked as if I had just bitten my grandmother and that this was one of my few pleasures, but all the rest were worse."*

IN the summer of 1952, as I've indicated, Flannery began to settle in at Andalusia. The next several years, up until the publication of her first collection of stories, *A Good Man Is Hard to Find*, were a time in which Flannery became reconciled to living in the South. She must have seen, as soon as she was well enough to start working again, that the routine of her life at Andalusia matched the schedule she had followed at Yaddo and with the Fitzgeralds. She had lived in New York City long enough to know that she far preferred country vistas to its rectilinear canyons. She had, in fact, chosen places in which to work that were Northern replicas of the farm: maples and ash had substituted for the pines; stone fences had compensated for red clay.

For her, of course, the Northern countryside was not invested with those memories that attach us to the places where we grow up, and that unite, by a kind of emotional prosthetics, the spirit and body of our life to the extensions, the limbs, of our region. This intimacy of the self with its homeland, an intimacy in which the distinction between the two tends to break down, has caused artists all kinds of problems, especially since the latter days of Romanticism. This intimacy is often seen as confining or even imprisoning. If the homeland is an extension of the self, the self ineluctably will be defined in part by its body. With his self-consciousness, the artist may feel himself to be a beautiful spirit buried within the ugly body of his homeland, forced like the mind of Frankenstein to identify itself with, perhaps, the ungainly gestures of chauvinism and the hunchback of racism. As a result, the artist usually tries to repeat the operation of his Creator, hoping for better results. He insists on being self-created, and to accomplish this he wanders the earth in search of a territory, a frame, that expresses what he wishes to be in his essence, thus making appearance and reality one. He does not want to be a freak. When O'Connor returned to the South, she was forced to live out what, from a late Romantic view, must have at first appeared to be a horror story. Imagine being isolated in long-forgotten Milledgeville, buried alive within the deep South! Joyce, at least physically, got clean away from Dublin; O'Connor was covered by the mire.

Yet we lovingly devote our attention now to every detail of life recorded by O'Connor. We yearn, because of her works, to have such a rich and magical homeland for our own. How did O'Connor effect this transition, first for herself and then for us?

O'Connor never expressed what we might call back-to-nature sentiments. The only thing she knew about the land, she claimed in an interview, was that it was underneath her. She was glad to let Regina have total control of the farm and openly resented depictions of her as "good country people"; she was "bourgeois," a term that more nearly corresponds in the South than in the rest of the country to its original meaning in French. She was also a woman who had made high art her milieu. So, although she found farm life a source of con-

stant entertainment and used her knowledge of it in her work, her relation to Andalusia and the surrounding country and its culture was never simple. "To know oneself is to know one's region," she wrote. "It is also to know the world, and it is also, paradoxically, a form of exile from that world" (*M & M*, p. 35). Her stories best illustrate the relation of this ensconced exile to her home, but the next-best illustration of it was the most homey activity she undertook: raising peacocks.

Peacocks are a kind of freak. They're not good for anything — one doesn't raise them to fry their eggs. Still, O'Connor's attachment to them was fierce. She wrote an essay about why she raised them in which she described the moment when the peacock unfurls its majestic tail:

> Frequently the cock combines the lifting of his tail with the raising of his voice. He appears to receive through his feet some shock from the center of the earth, which travels upward through him and is released: *Eee-ooo-ii! Eee-ooo-ii!* To the melancholy this sound is melancholy and to the hysterical it is hysterical. To me it has always sounded like a cheer for an invisible parade. (*M & M*, pp. 14-15)

The passage asks us implicitly to make a connection, to answer how the peacock's call qualifies O'Connor's state of mind. The answer expresses the individuality of a woman who learned to accept her vocation as an artist and the curious way in which her illness reinforced that vocation. Like the peacock, the artist too is a freak with one outsized attribute: the map of the universe to be found in his prophetic

Scenes of Andalusia. O'Connor enjoyed writing comic send-ups of "life on the farm" ("Me and Maw are still at the farm. . . . She is nuts about it out here, surrounded by the lowing herd and other details"). But she seems to have enjoyed rural living, in her way, as much as Regina did.

Andalusia was known for its peacocks, which O'Connor enjoyed raising because she found them both majestic and laughable. But she was also amused by the farm's population of donkeys. One Christmastime she wrote to a friend, "Equinox [the burro] has been invited to be in the Hardwick Christian Church's Christmas crib. We think we will send his papa, Ernest, instead, as Ernest is more liable to enter into the spirit of it. . . . I gave Ernest to my mother for a Mother's Day present two years ago. Somebody said that was for the mother who had everything. . . ."

imagination. He's not good for anything except to testify to the invisible parade, the procession of humanity as it marches into eternity. In one way he's only an adornment; the parade will go on without his calling attention to it. In another way his role is the quintessentially human one: to perform Adam's task, to praise God through naming the elements of creation. Thus man mysteriously brings the creation more completely into being; he is conscious of it as the animal kingdom cannot be. Thus, too, the artist creates his work, adds to the creation, and as he names his subcreation, he enables it to show forth its meaning and thus its glory — he transfigures it, as the peacock is transfigured in the action of spreading his tail.

To accomplish this the artist must do something that the peacock has no trouble doing but that mankind has a great deal of trouble with. He must accept the limitations of his own freakish nature. In "A Temple of the Holy Ghost," we saw a recollected image of Mary Flannery starting to understand this. In her raising of peacocks we have another affirmation of it. Care for animals — and here "husbandry" carries with it useful connotations — binds one to them, imposes limits: someone must put out their feed and help create conditions in which their offspring can survive. O'Connor's peacocks were a sign of her commitment to life at Andalusia, her way of saying this place was home.

In the same activity we also see her desire for transcendence through her interpretation of the peacock's call. She is at home at Andalusia, but only in a provisional way, as a place marker for the "home" that Hazel Motes finds at last: heaven (cf. *Wise Blood*, p. 231).

O'Connor wrote that she was afraid writers would always be glad of Christ's statement that "ye have the poor always with you," for the poor most directly express the pervasive character of each person's experience, its limitations. But rather than chafe against the restrictions of her illness, ever frustrated, O'Connor accepted the body of the place she was given to inhabit to the extent of accepting her illness. She did not do this in a stoic way, making the best of a bad fate, but in the hope of that transcendence to which she heard the peacock give its testimony. She looked to find her freedom not in escape — roaming the world as a ghost seeking the body of an ideal place to inhabit — but in acceptance, obedience. Perhaps she was helped in this personal motion of the heart by understanding its operation in her public role, her vocation as a writer:

> It is the peculiar burden of the fiction writer that he has to make one country do for all and that he has to evoke that one country through the concrete particulars of a life that he can make believable.
>
> This is first of all a matter of vocation, and a vocation is a limiting factor which extends even to the kind of material that the writer is able to apprehend imaginatively. The writer can choose what he writes about but he cannot choose what he is able to make live, and so far as he is concerned, a living deformed character is acceptable and a dead whole one is not. The Christian writer particularly will feel that whatever his initial gift is, it comes from God; and no matter how minor a gift it is, he will not be willing to destroy it by trying to use it outside its proper limits. (*M & M*, p. 27)

We can continue the parallel by saying that it is the peculiar — that is, the individual — burden of each person that one place will nearly always be *the* place in his experience. He may find its prosthetic extensions nothing but an encumbrance, but like a paralytic he must work at accepting this given, to receive it as from God's hands. This does not mean that God is responsible for the impaired character of the places we are given — man's disobedience is responsible for his expulsion from Eden. It does mean that the only way back into paradise is through the reversal of our original misdeed; instead of claiming our places, our gardens, as our own, we must put ourselves and our homelands at God's disposal. He is the author of creation; only he knows fully how to re-create it, redeem it. We help in this process by being at his service. By submitting ourselves to the truth of our bound conditions, we, paradoxically, find our freedom, just as an author in being as true as possible to the particular character of one experience finds a portal into universal truth and its freedom. This is unspeakably hard, of course. In the face of it we can only pray "Lord, have mercy." But for us a deformed life is better than death. We have to acknowledge even this impaired existence of ours as precious and work at its restoration by first accepting its limits, understanding that no home can be what we long for it to be: our place in God's kingdom.

Surely O'Connor's understanding of Christian obedience in her life also taught her about the nature of her vocation. I've used her thoughts about her work as a gloss of what she must have gone through in her soul. The opposite tack would be as valid; the two in-terpenetrate. Let the peacock stand as an emblem of her life in the same way that her fictions reveal the truth of her vocation. Trying in both to be obedient to the will of God, to accept her fate as from his hand, to preserve the gift and push it to its limits but not beyond them, O'Connor sought not the transcendence of escape but the transmutation of the limits' substance by the Refiner's fire. We cannot say much about the efficacy of this in her life; we can say that in her work we see a world transfigured, a world where every humble thing bears the weight of an immense glory — just as the peacock, a relative of the humble chicken, becomes almost another figure entirely when it is seen with the full glory of its tail unfolded. We treasure Flannery O'Connor's world because she learned to see it under the aspect of eternity. We are all given such places, but few of us have the eyes to see them.

O'Connor's return to the South, which in an imaginative sense she had hardly left, enriched her appreciation of her region dramatically. Living at Andalusia, she began writing stories that, although their seeds can be found in *Wise Blood*, might have been impossible for her to create if she had remained in the North. In one of Hazel Motes's sermons, O'Connor savages Gauguin's famous universal questions: Who are we? Where do we come from? Where are we going? At the same time, she sets out the conclusions that Nathanael West found true if unlivable, and shows the attitude toward the world and our places in it that necessarily follow: "No truth behind all truths is what I and this church preach! Where you come from is gone, where you thought you were going to never was there, and where you are is no good unless you can get away from it. Where is there a place for you to be? No place" (*WB*, p. 165).

There's a certain symbolical thinness to *Wise Blood*, a lack of gravity that shows when its characters lift toward allegory. Perhaps this is so simply because *Wise Blood* is a first novel. We can also entertain the possibility, however, that it reflects O'Connor's own flight from the truth of what *Wise Blood*, by way of implicit contrast, preaches: the rejection of Gauguin's flight to his Tahitian paradise and the other forms of escape pursued by his followers. Be that as it may, the stories O'Connor wrote from 1951 through 1955 (after she settled down at Andalusia), which are collected in *A Good Man Is Hard to Find*, have a gravity and fullness that the first novel lacks. The stories use the matter of place not simply as material for a wonderful harangue (nor simply for transparently symbolic gestures such as Haze's aborted escape from Taulkinham) but as the issue, what's at stake, at the heart of the stories themselves.

Nowhere is this more apparent than in "The Displaced Person," a story that can be treated as representative of all the stories in *A Good Man Is Hard to Find*. In certain respects "The Displaced Person" is not what many devoted readers of her work would consider inimitable O'Connor. The story is one of the few tragedies O'Connor ever wrote. Even stories as seemingly merciless as "A Good Man Is Hard to Find," "The River," and *Wise Blood* itself have to be considered tragicomedies: the grandmother who is murdered in "Good Man," the little boy who drowns in "The River," and Hazel Motes all arrive "home" in the end. (It

is an inimitable feature of O'Connor that she forces us as readers to place spiritual values before temporal ones in these crucifying, happy endings, and thereby tests our characters.) In addition, "The Displaced Person" sets us at a greater distance from its participants, and thus its ironies are broader and not quite as funny. Finally, the linchpin of the action has to do with racism, a topic that O'Connor tended to avoid in order that her fiction might not be read as disguised sociology. Keeping these differences in mind, we can appreciate "The Displaced Person" properly, and use it as a paradigm for the collection.

In "The Displaced Person" a priest, Father Flynn, has convinced Mrs. McIntyre, the owner of a dairy farm, that she should provide a job and a place to live for a Polish man and his family who have been displaced by World War II. The family arrives soon after Mrs. McIntyre has promised Father Flynn that she will help them. The Displaced Person, Mr. Guizac, quickly shows himself to be a hard and efficient worker. A skillful mechanic, carpenter, and mason, he upgrades the farm's operation in a noticeably short time. His presence causes dislocations in the hierarchical structure of the farm, however, and the other farmhands and then Mrs. McIntyre herself cross this good man's simple intentions. As these actions and counteractions loop around each other, the thatch, the knot, of the dramatic action develops. We see this in the first of the story's three sections through the eyes of Mrs. Shortley, the wife of Chancey Shortley, the white man who runs the dairy. Mrs. Shortley has been the farm's undisputed second-in-command until the arrival of the Guizacs, who threaten to displace her. Mrs. Shortley's anxiety about her place, her fear of her husband's being put out of work by the Guizacs, leads her finally to lose that place and, indeed, her very life. The point of view switches in the last two sections of the story, and we witness further events through Mrs. McIntyre's eyes. Although the Displaced Person's hard work makes her financial position more secure, his values threaten to undermine hers and in so doing jeopardize her role on the farm, her sovereignty over it.

O'Connor presents Mrs. Shortley (like all of her characters, ironically named) in monumental terms: "She stood on two tremendous legs, with the grand self-confidence of a mountain, and rose, up narrowing bulges of granite, to two icy blue points of light that pierced forward, surveying everything" (*CS*, p. 194). For her part, Mrs. Shortley believes — totally, it would seem — in the reality of appearances. She knows that she isn't white trash because she assumes that if she were, Mrs. McIntyre wouldn't talk about the workers who had preceded the Shortleys as trash. The stress that Mrs. Shortley feels after the arrival of the Displaced Person increases rather than diminishes her penchant for self-congratulation. At first she delights in menacing the blacks who work on the farm with the notion that the ten million Guizacs of the world may take their places. She sees herself as an archangel ushering the displaced multitudes in and the blacks out. But later, threatened herself with the same fate, she disguises her self-concern by taking up two roles: first she thinks of herself as the blacks' heroic protector, and then she becomes God's prophet. Her fantasies of self-aggrandizement move toward a satanic presumption.

Mrs. McIntyre appears to be just the opposite of Mrs. Shortley, a practical woman with real prerogatives and responsibilities. The information we have about her past tends to confirm our impression that she's a woman who knows what she wants and how to get it. Something of a fortune hunter, at thirty she married a seventy-year-old man, Judge McIntyre, who was reputed to be wealthy. As it turned out, his estate consisted of nothing more than the farm. Still, Mrs. McIntyre did have the pleasure of his company — she discovered that she enjoyed him — and did inherit the piece of property that she has maintained and that has supplied her needs for twenty years. The farm has seen her through two subsequent marriages that both ended in divorce. She has kept it a going business despite a catalogue of woes headed by a string of incompetent workers. Yet the very thing she was looking for in her first marriage — security — has eluded her. She is far from a comfortable member of the landed gentry; at bottom she feels like the poorest woman on earth. The people who look rich, she reasons, are the poorest because they have the most to keep up. In one way this is merely a dodge, an all-purpose rationalization for doing what she wants. She expresses what she believes to be a fundamental truth when she says, "This is my place. . . . I say who will come here and who won't" (*CS*, p. 223). But the story questions whether that statement is *the* fundamental truth of the matter, partly by showing us Mrs. McIntyre's timidity. She counts on a worker's quitting when she lets him know in roundabout ways that she finds him unsatisfactory, yet she has never actually fired anyone. And her fear is not simply irrational but springs from the real sense — no man or woman is an island — in which she is dependent on, at the mercy of, her workers. In addition, her responsibilities really do weigh her down; her litany of complaints finally convinces us that she is the poorest of the lot in the sense that she enjoys her farm less than anyone else on it. Her sovereignty limited, her satisfactions minimal, Mrs. McIntyre's ownership of the farm is entailed with questions. Her sense of her possession of it begins to resemble Mrs. Shortley's fanciful notions.

Mrs. McIntyre and Mrs. Shortley are one of the combative pairs that give rise to the conflict in many of O'Connor's stories. In *A Good Man Is Hard to Find* this pattern crops up in "The Life You Save May Be Your Own" (in Mr. Shiftlet's outfoxing Lucynell Crater), "A Circle in the Fire" (in Mrs. Pritchard and Mrs. Cope), "The Artificial Nigger" (in Mr. Head and Nelson), and in a double way in "Good Country People" (in Mrs. Hopewell and Mrs. Freeman and in Hulga and the Bible salesman). Outwardly friendly toward one another, the two in each pair are rivals, playing an endless game of one-upsmanship. They are locked in a dreadful battle for dominance. Often, as in the case of Mrs. McIntyre and Mrs. Shortley, the relationship is tainted by one figure's being the employee of the other; friendliness often gives way to force, albeit disguised, on the employer's part, and to dissembling on the employee's part. Those who are related — Mr. Head and Nelson, for instance, in "The Artificial Nigger" — resort to underlying claims of good intentions to keep the terrible truth of their relationship at bay. But the selfishness of these pairs, their desire for dominance over

each other, ends — unless somehow redeemed — in murderous hatred. Throughout her mature stories — in *A Good Man Is Hard to Find* and in the later collection, *Everything That Rises Must Converge* — O'Connor explores this form of evil, the plain mean-spiritedness of man, his selfishness and greed. O'Connor would certainly concur with Freud, although in a sense completed by her metaphysics, that man has a death instinct. As in Thomas Hardy's stories, most of the calamity between these combative pairs could be avoided if only the person who sins against the other would confess his fault.

The unwillingness to confess abounds in "The Displaced Person." Harboring the guilty secret of Chancey's moonshine still, Mrs. Shortley fails to make a relatively simple confession and amendment of life that would preserve what ostensibly she values above everything else: her position on the farm. Similarly, when Father Flynn argues with Mrs. McIntyre about keeping the Guizacs, Mrs. McIntyre fails to confess the real reason she suddenly wants to get rid of them: she says nothing about Mr. Guizac's soliciting help from one of the blacks to bring his cousin to the United States. (The black, Sulk, is to contribute half of the cousin's passage from Europe and then marry her, an arrangement that Mrs. McIntyre finds distasteful.) Mrs. McIntyre feeds the priest a series of excuses for getting rid of the Guizacs but never the racist reason. We cannot dominate those around us, the implied rationale has it, if we confess our weaknesses to them; ultimately, when we act on the same false motive before God, we are claiming that we are the lords of our territories. Thinking only of getting the best of each other, the combative pair exhibits pride that often — as it does here — excludes the intervention of God. Pride clutches the creation for itself, repeating Adam's original misdeed. Unwittingly, Mrs. McIntyre and Mrs. Shortley engage in combat that assumes hellish proportions.

The dimensions of Mrs. Shortley's presumption as well as that of Mrs. McIntyre become manifest in their attitudes toward the Displaced Person. How they read him determines how we read them. It also determines their fate.

Prior to the coming of the Displaced Person, Mrs. Shortley did not think of herself as someone who needed religion; strong people could avoid sin without it. But a sudden inspiration, lodged in a retort to Mrs. McIntyre that she should be suspicious of good fortune (the Displaced Person's work) that comes from the devil, aligns what heretofore has been a miscellany of prejudices into something like a system of thought, a religion. Mrs. Shortley remembers newsreel footage of the Holocaust, bodies piled on top of each other, and in her meditations on this image certain tenets of faith emerge. The tragedy of World War II and its Holocaust must have come to Europe, she reasons, because society there isn't as advanced as it is in the peaceful United States. Its backwardness is coupled in her mind with what she takes for its pervasive religion, Roman Catholicism, a faith that hasn't had its primitive errors reformed out of it. But seeing that Mr. Guizac has more technical expertise than her Chancey, Mrs. Shortley must abandon the relatively innocuous notion of progress as the ground of her superiority. In the process Catholicism shifts from being an attendant ill to

the cause of everything wrong with the Guizacs. The Guizacs and their religion are no longer merely backward — they are evil. Their faith carries the evil virus that brought about the plague of the Holocaust. Perhaps, Mrs. Shortley worries, they will transmit this disease to America. Soon, with the Guizacs' threat to the Shortleys' employment plain, she becomes convinced that Europe must indeed be the devil's experiment station. Mr. Guizac is unquestionably from the devil, and he and his family and those like him are coming to America to establish the Whore of Babylon in the temple of America. Reading her Bible, especially the Prophets and Revelation, Mrs. Shortley becomes convinced that she has been called to prophesy against this evil, to wage a holy war against it — which will of course justify what she really wants to do: get rid of the Guizacs before they supplant her family. Simple chauvinism has thus turned into pharisaical religion. (We should be reminded that Christ was accused of being from Beelzebub by the Pharisees of his day.)

A similar shift occurs in Mrs. McIntyre's thinking about the Guizacs, although it takes much longer to develop. The seeds of the Displaced Person's virtue never take root in the hardpan soul of Mrs. Shortley, but they do shoot up in Mrs. McIntyre's soul before being choked by weeds and tares. At first Mrs. McIntyre cannot quite believe that her scheming kindness in giving the Guizacs work to do and a place to live has brought her the grace of such an exemplary worker. His presence doesn't seem altogether real; he is too much a "miracle." But she does understand the implications of his being on the farm: she tells Mrs.

Shortley that the Displaced Person will be her "salvation" (CS, p. 203). Even Mrs. Shortley can see the wondrous effect the Displaced Person has on Mrs. McIntyre; she acts like "somebody who was getting rich secretly" (CS, p. 208). Mrs. McIntyre's faith grows enough for her to buy Mr. Guizac a silage cutter, a drag harrow, and a tractor with a power lift. She looks forward to a future untroubled by the necessity of riding herd on her workers; she will be free of that anxiety at last.

As long as Mrs. McIntyre accepts the wealth of the Displaced Person's grace without quibbling over the terms by which it has been granted, she lives a new life. The instincts of her old life have not died within her, however, and she soon wants to turn the gift of the Displaced Person into a possession. She worries about paying him just enough for him to stay but not so much that he'll eventually have the means to move up in society. (She thinks that the Guizacs are getting fat when the hollows have gone out of their cheeks.) She keeps insisting that she has finally found a man who *has* to work, taking comfort in necessity. Her original nature, her fortune-hunting self, has not changed; she still wants to be secure, to save her own life. But he that will save his life shall lose it. Grace, being freely given, must be freely received. Constraints banish it. Without knowing it, Mrs. McIntyre has already started to pull at the flaw that will give way and pitch the farm back into its old life. She does not recognize that the flaw lies within her own soul, that the desire to seize control and security for herself will always undo whatever agents of grace appear. She wants granary bins for God's manna and doesn't see the contradiction in terms. Her possessiveness will surely make her forfeit her possessions.

The occasion that tears asunder Mrs. McIntyre's salvation, and eventually crucifies it in the person of Mr. Guizac, has nothing in it of necessity — although we have to remind ourselves of this. Mr. Guizac, as noted, involves Sulk in his plan to bring his cousin to America. Mrs. McIntyre immediately despairs of keeping the Guizacs after her confused, angry explanation to the Displaced Person of why he cannot carry out his plan. Unless we have felt the anxiety building within Mrs. McIntyre, understood her possessiveness, we may miss a good deal of the story's meaning, chalking up the impasse to racism. Mrs. McIntyre is certainly a racist, and O'Connor wants us to condemn racism, but she also wants us to see racism as one mode of a larger evil: pride. Mrs. McIntyre's pride is built on her false sense of ruling the farm. When she confronts Mr. Guizac about the proposed marriage between his cousin and Sulk, she makes race the issue, but she is really stressing her control over the farm — and the control she feels she has a right to exercise over Mr. Guizac. When she talks to Father Flynn soon after, she insists that Mr. Guizac must go, not because he is unsatisfactory, as she claims, but because she wants to "say who will come here and who won't." In both instances she is hiding from herself what her anger and her tyrannical pronouncements reveal: she resents Mr. Guizac's independence. She recognizes that she will never be able to control him — not as she controls her black workers, nor to the extent that she has controlled her white help — no matter how hard she rides him. Mr. Shortley knows the truth: if Mrs. McIntyre banishes the Guizacs from the farm, Mr. Guizac will become such a success in business that he'll own a house and a TV set within three years. Mrs. McIntyre knows this, too. But instead of accepting the limits of her power and being thankful for what the Guizacs will have accomplished, she blames the world — and, by implication, God — for the difficulties of this situation and, indeed, of her life, for which we now see she alone is responsible.

I've been using heavy theological language, implying at every turn that Mrs. Shortley's and Mrs. McIntyre's relationships with the Displaced Person are images of their relationships to God in Christ. But I've taken my cue from O'Connor. She makes it quite clear that Mr. Guizac is a Christ figure. We are given little specific information about him. We are told that his smile shows teeth missing on one side, and that the black workers, because of their slow pace, make him nervous. Otherwise, even his face is described as a composite of several others (*CS*, p. 222). When he is referred to as the "Displaced Person," the first letter of each word in the epithet is always capitalized. When Mrs. McIntyre argues with Father Flynn about whether the Guizacs will stay, she thinks she has forever silenced the priest's appeal to Christ by what she believes is the blasphemous admission that Christ was just another displaced person (*CS*, p. 229). Of course he was. His kingdom was not of this world, and the children of men proved it by crucifying him. "The Son of Man hath nowhere to lay his head" (Matt. 8:20) — Christ has no place in this world, no habitation, except as his grace is received into the lives of those who believe on him.

Mrs. Shortley, true to her name, rejects the Displaced Person out-of-hand. Mrs. McIntyre, unable to cage the tyger burning bright, turns on him. In a sense there's really no need for O'Connor to make pretenses about Mr. Guizac's being a Christ figure. She might well argue that the image of Christ is always present in the poor, and she has not introduced a symbol so much as polished a ubiquitous image, an image that does not simply refer to Christ but bears him, carries his immanent presence into the life of the farm to be the life of the farm. When Mrs. McIntyre tells Father Flynn that there's "no Christ our Lord" on the farm (*CS*, p. 231), she's dead wrong. He is in her world but not of it. He is the artificial nigger, God casting himself — using the devices of the incarnational art that belongs first to him — in the form of a man. He, as Mrs. McIntyre says of the Displaced Person, "doesn't fit in" (*CS*, p. 225) because he explodes the bounds of our small meanness. In one of her final verbal judgments of the Displaced Person, Mrs. McIntyre says, "He's extra and he's upset the balance around here" (*CS*, p. 231). It is a clear echo of the misfit's observation in "A Good Man Is Hard to Find": "Jesus thown everything off balance" (*CS*, p. 131).

After the displaced person has proven his worth, Mrs. Shortley overhears that Mrs. McIntyre intends to fire Chancey. In response she marshals her family's energies, and they stage a quick retreat. They pack all their belongings in and on top of their car and leave at sunrise of the next day. Their rivalry almost over, Mrs. Shortley can't abide the exercise of Mrs. McIntyre's sovereignty; she'd rather quit than be fired. Her friendship with Mrs. Mc-

Intyre and her assumption of the roles of protecting archangel and prophet have been the superstitious ways by which she has maintained her illusion of superiority to Mrs. McIntyre. She acts to preserve something of these illusions, whatever the cost.

The circumstances of Mrs. Shortley's final departure and the language in which they are described fittingly bring to its apotheosis the greatest illusion in Mrs. Shortley's life. On Sunday afternoon, just before Mrs. Shortley overhears Mrs. McIntyre voice her intentions, she has a vision while driving in the cows for Chancey. Walking often triggers distressful physical symptoms in Mrs. Shortley: "At times she could feel her heart, like a child's fist, clenching and unclenching inside her chest" (*CS*, p. 210). But on this afternoon she is walking without pain when she sees a "gigantic figure" with "fiery wheels with fierce dark eyes in them, spinning rapidly all around it" (*CS*, p. 210). The figure commands her to prophesy, and she does, eyes shut and fists clenched. " 'The children of the wicked nations will be butchered,' she said in a loud voice. 'Legs where arms should be, foot to face, ear in the palm of hand. Who will remain whole? Who will remain whole? Who?' " (*CS*, p. 210). These pronouncements come true but far from the way that Mrs. Shortley hopes they will. Indeed, the essential genius of the story — and this is true of much of O'Connor's work — is that *everything* in it is true. Its ironic elements don't reverse the story's direction but contribute to the forward action. Yet, like the current from a muddy tributary when a river is on the rise, the darkness of the irony can be distinguished, in retrospect, from the other currents of the story by the clarity, the purification of

this river, to which the action of the story finally brings us. In other words, the story operates on two planes, the true and the ironically true, and the action teaches us how the two planes interpret each other.

Mrs. Shortley's prophecy is painfully self-fulfilled when she and her family leave the farm. They are sandwiched into the car amid their belongings, and Mrs. Shortley's position in the car is described in a way that reminds us of her earlier memory of newsreel footage of Holocaust victims: "Mrs. Shortley sat with one foot on a packing box so that her knee was pushed into her stomach. Mr. Shortley's elbow was almost under her nose and Sarah Mae's [her daughter's] bare left foot was sticking over the front seat, touching her ear" (*CS*, p. 213). Volcanic heat and pressure have been building in Mrs. Shortley since she heard that Chancey was to receive his notice, and a deadly eruption, a stroke, precipitates a strange fit before it kills her: "She suddenly grabbed Mr. Shortley's elbow and Sarah Mae's foot at the same time and began to tug and pull on them as if she were trying to fit the two extra limbs onto herself. . . . She thrashed forward and backward, clutching at everything she could get her hands on and hugging it to herself" (*CS*, p. 213).

This child "of the wicked nations," of the kingdom of darkness, does not remain whole. In this last frantic scene legs go "where arms should be," Sarah Mae's foot is in Mrs. Shortley's face, someone's ear is in the palm of her hand — all because her heart, her desires, have been "clutching" everything within reach her life long. We are told that her children — who keep asking at the moment of her death, "Where we goin, Ma?" — didn't understand that she had "ever been displaced in the world from all that belonged to her" (*CS*, p. 214). She has been displaced from the farm by her own actions (Mrs. McIntyre has never fired anyone, and it's unlikely that she would have carried out her intention to fire the Shortleys). She has been displaced from her very life by her hatred of the Displaced Person. Even more at the heart of the matter, her attempts to appropriate a position a cut above Mrs. McIntyre through emotional magic have all along placed her in an unreal world. Hers has been a living death; her poverty has grown in direct proportion to her claims otherwise. Wanting to be an archangel or a prophet has caused her to forfeit what truly did belong to her: her genuine love for her husband and her children. She cannot answer the girls' question now, and never could in a fundamental sense, because instead of accepting the place assigned to her she has preferred the "no place" of self-aggrandizing fantasies. When she dies, her eyes, "like blue-painted glass, seemed to contemplate for the first time the tremendous frontiers of her true country" (*CS*, p. 214). The tone of the line seems to suggest that in death she has finally found life: she understands, perhaps, that when God becomes our sovereign, we can then take our rightful place in our "true country." For our longings to belong to a homeland and a home are themselves displaced yearnings for a place that's to be found not in this world but the next.

Shortly after this incident, Mrs. McIntyre, unable to enslave the Guizacs in her accustomed manner, looks toward banishing them from the farm. The return of Chancey Shortley after an interval gives her further encourage-

ment to do so. She finds herself grieving for the loss of Mrs. Shortley, whom she once again thinks of as a good friend. Remembering the woman's sentiments about the Guizacs, she laments not seeing the reason in Mrs. Shortley's logic earlier. Without a sign of her usual irritation with help who express their opinions, she lets Mr. Shortley babble away about the injustice of having fought for the principle that all men are created equal only to find himself displaced by his former, unequal enemy. Yet here a curious dissolution takes place — takes *the* place of Mrs. McIntyre. As I've noted, the story opens with Mrs. McIntyre and the reader sharing presumptions about ownership, but the story gradually exhausts these presumptions. In the process the figure of Mrs. McIntyre is scaled down to barely more than a cipher. Though she plans to dismiss Mr. Guizac, occasion after occasion goes by without her confronting him. She finally sails out to tell him, but her first attempt ends with her having railed about her obligations and bills and having said nothing about firing the Displaced Person.

Mrs. McIntyre's second attempt gets rid of Mr. Guizac through a violence that bespeaks her lack of control, her powerlessness. Standing by the small tractor while Mr. Guizac lies half-under the machine, making repairs, Mrs. McIntyre watches Chancey drive the larger tractor out of the barn. He parks it directly in line with them on the grade above. The parking brake slips, and the monstrous machine rolls toward the place where Mr. Guizac lies. No one calls out a warning. Just before the tractor reaches Mr. Guizac's prone form, Mrs. McIntyre, Mr. Shortley, and Sulk look at one another, and this look forever seals the trinity's collusion in the murder. Letting the out-of-control tractor crush Mr. Guizac, they show their hollow pride is similarly out of control. Mrs. McIntyre does not have the courage to say who comes and who goes on her place, nor even the will to go against the wishes of Father Flynn, who has been lobbying for her to keep the Displaced Person. She is caught in a dilemma of her own making. Consequently, she forfeits her habitation, her place:

> She looked first at his [the Displaced Person's] bloody pants legs and then at his face which was not averted from her but was as withdrawn and expressionless as the rest of the countryside. She only stared at him for she was too shocked by her experience to be quite herself. Her mind was not taking hold of all that was happening. She felt she was in some foreign country where the people bent over the body were natives, and she watched like a stranger while the dead man was carried away in the ambulance. (*CS*, p. 235)

The Displaced Person has become native to the countryside, while she, obstinately blind to the needs of a world where people suffer, has placed herself in a limbo of impotent selfishness. Mrs. Shortley and she are not opposites but inverted images of each other, zero over zero. She too has made her dwelling in unreality. The poor will inherit the kingdom of heaven — their suffering will be recompensed — but the rich have their reward already. The harder they clutch it to themselves, the more they smother its life. O'Connor seems to be saying that if we insist on being the sovereigns of our worlds rather than their stewards, we will lose even the provisional sense in which we are at home in this world. For we are all displaced people, exiles from Eden. Only in Christ, the second Adam, can we find our place: "For in him we live, and move, and have our being" (Acts 17:28). The story concludes with Mrs. McIntyre's experiencing physical problems that are signs of her failing the spiritual test she was put to. She loses her health: her eyesight worsens, her voice fails, her head and hands begin "to jiggle" (*CS*, p. 235). No longer able to run the farm and having lost all her help, Mrs. McIntyre's only substantial contact with the world comes through Father Flynn, who remembers to visit her and carry on her instruction in the church's teaching.

A Good Man Is Hard to Find was in one way a great critical success; at least it was highly praised. Two "laws" of literary life apparently played a part in its reception: the law of compensation and the law of momentum. *Wise Blood* lingered in the collective mind, alive despite its supposed weaknesses. In time the grounds on which it had been faulted looked erroneous and the arguments against it specious. As critics had emphasized the hypothetical sins of *Wise Blood*, they now repented by drawing attention to the virtues of the collection. Then, too, the stories in *A Good Man* had been appearing in magazines and literary journals, and the process of individual publication and then collection gave the literati time to reflect on the author's progress and make it in their own minds something like a procession. This gathering sense of O'Connor's importance helped make the reviews function like news bulletins on O'Connor's election to the pantheon of contemporary writers. *Why* she was important was still very much in dispute.

Another two years passed before O'Connor declared the absolute relevance of her "orthodox Christianity" to her work. She did so in a reflective piece called "The Fiction Writer and His Country," which Granville Hicks requested for *The Living Novel: A Symposium*. The subsequent horror, in some quarters of the literary community, at having already elevated this living anachronism, this Christian, to a place of honor shows how few rightly understood *A Good Man Is Hard to Find*. As late as November 1961, O'Connor was still explaining to John Hawkes, her friend and a fellow novelist, that she was not, as he kept insisting, on the devil's side in her work. She finally declared that while his devil was the enemy of the bourgeois, her devil had "a name, a history and a definite plan. His name is Lucifer, he's a fallen angel, his sin is pride, and his aim is the destruction of the Divine plan" (*Letters*, p. 456).

*   *   *

Fittingly, the success of *A Good Man Is Hard to Find* brought with it a partial remedy to misconceived notions about O'Connor's work. She was invited to speak by a variety of groups — women's clubs and civic organizations as well as colleges and universities. Aided by Merticorten and her crutches, O'Connor was now able to travel, and she accepted many such engagements. These occasions drew out (we might better say "provoked") her own view of the nature of fiction. Eliot said that a writer is always arguing for his way of doing things when he makes critical remarks, and this could not have

been more true than in O'Connor's case. In these talks she made it clear that her vision was Christian and Catholic — for her the two were entirely synonymous — and that she found within Thomism, principally as expressed in Jacques Maritain's *Art and Scholasticism*, the best statement on aesthetics of what she knew to be true in practice. She worked and reworked the ideas closest to her own experience as her knowledge of them grew — adapting them to suit particular audiences — and ended up producing reams of speeches. As a result, Robert and Sally Fitzgerald were able to collect her formal essays, extract a number of others from the manuscripts of her speeches, and publish them together in *Mystery & Manners*. O'Connor's novels and stories must stand by themselves, but in the same way that O'Connor used Christian dogma as an interpretive guide to what she saw, so the reader can use her critical remarks as an aid to experiencing her fiction. The critical directions the essays suggest help us detect the signs that lead us in the pathways of the stories. The trails are there whether or not we've read the essays, of course. But when we return to the fiction after reading the essays, we are usually shocked at how we have missed the obvious.

O'Connor came to prefer reading her work to talking about it. I've heard a tape of one such reading. On it O'Connor makes prefatory remarks and then proceeds with "A Good Man Is Hard to Find." Her voice sounds breathy at first, so much so that I thought of Southern belles. But as the story progresses, her voice has the heat of emotion in it, which evaporizes the wet vowels of her accent. When The Misfit, a mass murderer, finally speaks, the snarl in O'Connor's voice is convincing: she sounds like she grew up in prison. She confided to a correspondent that she could be a real ham, and kidded about rivaling the famous readings of Dickens. The recording testifies to her fine ear for dialogue, and the uncanny performance reminds us of her "wanting the people but not getting them." But that was changing.

Her letters reveal a nexus of reasons for her acceptance of these invitations as well as her reservations about them. She was the kind of person, she wrote, who liked to be in distant places but did not enjoy getting there. With her health and a more nervous disposition than she let show, traveling must have taken it out of her. She was also dismayed at some of the responses — from oversophisticated to stupid — that she met to her work. She didn't make much light conversation; she once suggested that "whoever invented the cocktail party should have been drawn and quartered" (*Letters*, p. 329). Yet she kept saying yes to the invitations to appear, even though the speeches siphoned off energy she might have put into her fiction. She enjoyed making money in this way and the opportunity the readings afforded to visit with the few literary people she found congenial. In addition, she was genuinely concerned about engendering love for the arts in people of faith, and she cared about the students she met on these trips. She was particularly moved by a conversation she had with a young woman after she gave a speech at Notre Dame:

> After it a girl came up to me and said, "I'm not a Catholic, I'm a Lutheran but you've given me some hope for the first time that Catholic writers may do something." I said, "Well please pray that we will." And she said, "I will, I will

in Christ." And she meant it and she will and it is that kind of thing that makes these trips worth the effort. (*Letters*, p. 216)

O'Connor responded in a similar way through correspondence to Alfred Corn, a student who was struggling to believe. She told this student that Gerard Manley Hopkins had answered Robert Bridges' question as to how he might know God with the instruction "Give alms." God is to be known more through charity than through the intellect operating in a Cartesian vacuum. Her speaking forays were, in part, her way of following this advice (*Letters*, p. 214). Unable to follow the common practices of devotion like fasting, she gave alms by enduring the hardships of travel and by bearing with people who misunderstood her.

Her pilgrimage in this world took an unlikely turn in 1958 when she traveled first to Lourdes and then on to Rome, where she was part of a group that had an audience with Pope Pius XII. Her cousin Katie, who paid for the trip, had prodded Regina and Flannery into taking it. At first they were to participate in a tour, but when the doctor advised against the rigors of nonstop sight-seeing, an adjusted itinerary was arranged for Flannery and her mother. Initially Flannery took a jaundiced view of going to Lourdes. She resisted the trip and was glad when the doctor's advice appeared to have canceled it, but she finally agreed to go, although she remained somewhat vexed. Theoretically, she believed in miracles, but having been sick for eight years, she must have regarded the notion of a miraculous cure as a kind of insult, an event that would make little of her suffering by predicating it, in retrospect, on grounds of insufficient faith. Flannery determined that she would go to Lourdes as a visitor, not a patient. If she was going to pray for a miracle at all, it would be for the grace to finish her novel-in-progress, *The Violent Bear It Away*.

But Sally Fitzgerald, who accompanied the party, did convince Flannery to bathe in and drink the water from the shrine's spring with the rest of *"les malades."* In an editorial note in the *Letters* Fitzgerald responds to a letter in which Flannery, tongue in cheek, claimed that Sally persuaded her to take the cure because she suffered from a "hyper-thyroid moral imagination." Fitzgerald says she forced Flannery into cooperating because she knew Flannery would feel guilty later for disappointing her cousin Katie. Fitzgerald believes, in fact, that Flannery wanted her to go along on the trip to perform just this service of persuasion (*Letters*, p. 282).

Fitzgerald seems to have been right. Not only was Flannery glad she had participated in the healing ceremony for her cousin's sake, but she also liked to think that the subsequent recalcification of her hipbones had something to do with her visit (see *Letters*, p. 305). Her faith shared something with Augustine's: evidences of the supernatural played little part in her faith early on, but became more prominent as she aged. In the letters from her last years we can sense a loosening up of sensibilities; she does not seem so concerned about adopting a low-profile spirituality for the sake of her intellectual friends.

Whether Lourdes had something to do with the recalcifying of her hipbones is a matter of conjecture — Flannery's own faith in this idea seems to have declined as her condition eventually began to deteriorate again. Certainly, however, she was given the grace to finish *The Violent Bear It Away*, a miracle of its own order.

The Violent Bear It Away

*T*HE *Violent Bear It Away* has a very different feel from that of the first two books. *The Violent Bear It Away* has nothing of the symbolical thinness of *Wise Blood*. The second novel also contains little of the daily and the routine, which *A Good Man Is Hard to Find* uses to convey its sense of place. *The Violent Bear It Away* has an immediacy and a vivacity that at once place its world around us, yet, in contrast to *A Good Man*, its power to do so carries with it an ever-present sense of menace. The stories in *A Good Man* contain sudden instances of violence in the otherwise stable lives of their characters; *The Violent Bear It Away* delivers us to a world in which there's no letup, a world in which everything seems to be at stake at every moment. If we can daydream about working Mrs. McIntyre's farm, we will often want to awaken from this novel, in which violence is a condition of being.

As with much of O'Connor's work, the almost visceral experience of reading the novel must seem disproportionate to a simple statement of its action. In a certain way even less happens in *The Violent Bear It Away* than in *Wise Blood*. Old Tarwater is a prophet who makes his living on his backwoods farm by operating a still. The story begins at the breakfast table, where he dies from a stroke or a heart attack. Old Tarwater has raised his grandnephew, also called Tarwater, to succeed him as a prophet, comparing their relationship to that of Elijah

and Elisha. Old Tarwater has also made the fourteen-year-old promise to carry out a last request: young Tarwater is to bury him ten — not eight — feet under, and put a cross at the head of his grave. Another voice, that of a stranger who in a short while we recognize as the devil, intercedes with objections to this commandment. (The devil will accompany Tarwater from here on out, growing in influence as the book progresses.) Forsaking his part in the covenant, abandoning his burial duties, Tarwater heeds the devil's urging and gets drunk on the old man's whiskey, then falls asleep. When he awakens, he burns down the farmhouse and in so doing believes he has cremated Old Tarwater, directly contradicting the old man's wishes.

Tarwater then escapes to the city and the home of his Uncle Rayber. At this point some background has to be sketched in, and O'Connor does it through extended flashbacks. When Rayber was seven years old, old Tarwater kidnapped him from his disbelieving parents and took him out to his farm, Powderhead, where he instructed Rayber in the facts of his redemption. Eventually taken back to the city by his father, Rayber nevertheless believed what old Tarwater had taught him and continued to think of himself as a Christian for some years. Eventually, however, he lost his faith. When Rayber's unbelieving parents and his sister, young Tarwater's mother, were killed in a car crash, old Tarwater moved in with Rayber (who by then was an adult), hoping to reconvert him. Rayber, a schoolteacher, listened to the old man, but only for the purpose of writing an article about him, thus reducing the old man's prophetic calling to neurotic delusion. When old Tarwater read the published article, he kidnapped young Tarwater, vowing to raise him up to be a prophet who would burn Rayber's eyes clean. Thus young Tarwater's return to his uncle carries on the contest for his soul between old Tarwater and Rayber.

At Rayber's house Tarwater meets Bishop, Rayber's retarded son. Another piece of background information is relevant here: old Tarwater, frustrated by Rayber in his efforts to baptize the dim-witted child himself, had enjoined young Tarwater to perform the rite as his first prophetic act. The heart of the book concerns whether Tarwater will finally choose belief or unbelief, as manifested in the litmus test of baptizing Bishop. Everything in the book rests on this baptism — not an issue we would imagine a contemporary author could make compelling.

Yet it is. Unlike other art novels — *To the Lighthouse* by Virginia Woolf, for instance — the novel somehow has pace. Something weighty is being advanced in every line, and we race to find out what it is. But that "it," that meaning, will elude us if we depend on the bones of the action itself for revelation. Indeed, simply to understand, in the fullest sense, *what* happens, we will have to understand *how* it happens. This calls for reading the novel with the strictest attention, as we read poetry. For the novel works, what happens happens, as

much like poetry as conventional prose narrative.

Like a good poem, *The Violent Bear It Away* has a consistent system of imagery. Its poetic radicals, the images that appear again and again in various forms, are surprisingly few: fire, water, hunger (and its object, bread), silence, the city, and the country. We have to attend to their appearance because the transformations they undergo carry the novel's weight of meaning. This action of poetic association does not merely provide a commentary on the events of the novel, because the action of the novel takes place in the rendering of it: description is made one with event.

As I've suggested, the poetic structure of the novel almost entirely replaces the machinery of conventional prose narrative. We can see this best in the case of Bishop's baptism. In most prose narrative we are always waiting to see what happens next — whether Robinson Crusoe will survive, or whether Isabel Archer, in Henry James's *Portrait of a Lady*, will make a good marriage. This applies, as I've indicated, to *The Violent Bear It Away* — we want to know what's going to happen — but in terms of the action alone O'Connor seems to subvert our wish rather than gratify it. The crux of the matter, that litmus test, is whether Tarwater will baptize Bishop. But then the event to which all others lead becomes itself problematic: Tarwater drowns the child, but he also recites the words of the baptismal rite at the same time. O'Connor compounds our difficulty by having this key scene take place offstage: we are given Rayber's imagining of the event at a distance and Tarwater's distorted re-experiencing of it in a dream. And yet, how O'Connor views the baptism/drowning remains the crux of the matter, for we can't help seeing that Tarwater's subsequent actions are determined (although he resists admitting this to himself) by what he has done to — and possibly for — Bishop. Authorial commentary on the matter would be extremely helpful, but we are supplied with almost none. We are left to study the novel's detail.

O'Connor takes great care to establish that detail, asking comparatively little of her audience in terms of general knowledge. We are told that the trials that have come to old Tarwater in his calling as a prophet have burned him clean. He has "learned by fire" (*VB*, p. 5). In his first efforts as a prophet, he "proclaimed from the midst of his fury that the world would see the sun burst in blood and fire" (*VB*, p. 5). Nothing came to pass, however, until one morning, "he saw to his joy a finger of fire coming out of it [the sun] . . . [which] had touched him and the destruction he had been waiting for had fallen in his own brain and his own body. His own blood had been burned dry and not the blood of the world" (*VB*, pp. 5-6). The statement of the third-person narrator — "He had learned enough to hate the destruction that had to come and not all that was going to be destroyed" — sounds right: it convinces us of the man's wisdom, and it validates his fiery vision (*VB*, p. 6). On the heels of this we are told that those times when old Tarwater thrashed out his peace with the Lord, he returned to young Tarwater looking "as if his head were still full of visions he had seen . . . wheels of light and strange beasts with giant wings of fire" (*VB*, p. 8). Later we are reminded of the burning bush, the sign of God's

presence given to Moses. If we do not hereafter equate fire and light with the presence of God and the gift of prophecy, it isn't O'Connor's fault. The importance of water (and thus baptism) is established in a similar way, as are the values of the other poetic radicals.

The ending of the novel brings these images to their consummation; they break apart like seeds and grow into the forms from which they derive. The planting of these seeds takes place all along the way, and there's a discernible root system that develops before the growth at the end.

By using an image repeatedly, O'Connor foreshadows the novel's denouement. This is particularly evident in the case of water imagery because O'Connor employs it in surprising contexts. When, after burning down Powderhead, Tarwater telephones Rayber on the way to his house, Bishop answers the phone. He cannot speak — he's that severely retarded — but Tarwater hears the distinctive sound of his breathing: "It was a kind of bubbling noise, the kind of noise someone would make who was struggling to breathe in water" (*VB*, p. 83). Water again figures in a description when Rayber remembers his father's coming to Powderhead and striding across a field to reclaim him after old Tarwater had kidnapped and baptized him. Because his conversion under the instruction of old Tarwater had been quite real and he hadn't wanted to go back to his family, the child Rayber had "let himself imagine that the field had an undertow that would drag his father backwards and suck him under" (*VB*, p. 126). When he revisits Powderhead with Bishop, Rayber again feels the force of divine love, which, after his falling away from the faith, has been centered completely in Bishop. At Powderhead he knows that if he were to lose Bishop, "the whole world would become his idiot child" (*VB,* p. 182). He tries to banish thoughts of the impossible demands of such a love, but they keep returning to his mind one by one: "He felt a sinister pull on his consciousness, the familiar *undertow* of expectation, as if he were still a child waiting on Christ" (*VB,* p. 182; italics mine).

The undertow has become sinister even though Tarwater at one time found hope in its force. The image itself gives us the key as to why: an undertow sometimes takes its victim to his death. Some understanding of Christian imagery is also helpful in connecting all the dots. The lowering of the baptismal candidate into water (or the sprinkling of water that has replaced immersion in most communions) symbolizes the person's dying to his evil nature. It unites his individual death with Christ's death on the cross, and allows the life-in-death of his faith, the ongoing denial of his sinful nature, to participate in the redemption of Christ.

In this frame Tarwater's simultaneous baptism and drowning of Bishop begins to make sense. The rite has a binary nature, involving first death and then rebirth in Christ. We must presume that Bishop — the focal point of divine love for Rayber and a child, as old Tarwater announces, who is precious in the sight of the Lord — goes straight to heaven. Here again O'Connor is employing her favorite strategy, reawakening us to the reality of neglected imagery by making it literal, by using it as what it claims to be: true in fact.

This insight in turn leads us back into the text — is in fact the crucial point of entry — in order to understand passages that may be opaque on a first reading. We will probably understand that Tarwater, urged by the stranger's voice to abandon digging old Tarwater's grave and get drunk, has been seduced by the devil. Still, his burning down his home and striking out for the city may come as a shock. We have to read carefully to see that he acts as he does because, upon awaking, he sees "a pink unsteady moon that appeared to be jerked up a foot or so and then dropped and jerked up again. This was because, as he observed in an instant, the sky was lowering, coming down fast to *smother* him" (*VB,* p. 49; italics mine). The word *smothered* implies asphyxiation and connects with the undertow and its consequence, drowning. Having forsaken his appointed task, Tarwater feels guilty, and so he experiences the death of Christ as judgment; and indeed, one of the horrors of the Cross is that it makes us face the terrible evil that lies within us. Instead of accepting this judgment, Tarwater tries simply to get rid of it, to destroy the accusatory image of his broken covenant, Powderhead. Yet the silver eyes of his grandfather will follow after him, glaring at his wrongdoing, accusing him.

We should also note that every time Tarwater feels that undertow pulling him toward Christ, images of immersion and its disorienting effect flood the narrative. When Tarwater knows absolutely — at least for a moment — that he has indeed been called to baptize Bishop, his protests are "*saturated* in silence, *lost*" (*VB,* p. 91; italics mine). Likewise, while he stays with Rayber, each time he is tempted to baptize Bishop, "he would feel that the silence was about to surround him and he was going to be *lost* in it forever" (*VB*, p. 160; italics mine). As we become aware of this pattern of imagery, the story takes on an inevitability that would be impossible otherwise. We usually speak of foreshadowing in terms of a small gesture, a telltale sign like a momentary reticence on the part of one character or another's flickering eyelid. Foreshadowing prepares us for a fiction's outcome; it stands as a sign of good faith that the author has not held back vital information. (The author always withholds some information, of course, but we at least want the sense that he has led us to his ending, not transported us there through the telekinesis of tricked-up art.) But the foreshadowing lodged in these images of immersion and drowning do more. At the end of many of the Sherlock Holmes mysteries, Holmes explains to Watson or the assembled members of the violent country weekend how he put two and two together. In a novel such as *The Violent Bear It Away*, we are presented a narrative without any of that kind of commentary; the experience of the story hits us in the compacted form of concrete imagery. Yet at the same time, we realize, the clues are there to be read. O'Connor describes, foreshadows, and advances the novel's action all at the same time. This makes possible a tremendous compression, the book's vision residing in each image, each mirroring pearl. We shall see that for this reason we can take up any one of the poetic radicals and, in the course of investigating it, unlock this treasure chest of a novel.

This pattern of imagery also lets O'Connor express the emotional life of a character in terms of the way he sees the world. We do have some discursive passages about how Rayber feels about Bishop and his life, but we have very little of this kind of discussion about Tarwater. We know how he feels mostly by how he looks at the world; in what he sees we see the correlatives of his thoughts and emotions. We find an example of this when Tarwater arrives at his Uncle Rayber's house. Tarwater sits on his uncle's front steps before letting anyone know of his arrival.

> He did not look up at the sky but he was unpleasantly aware of the stars. They seemed to be holes in his skull through which some distant unmoving light was watching him. It was as if he were alone in the presence of an immense silent eye. He had an intense desire to make himself known to the schoolteacher at once, to tell him what he had done and why and to be congratulated by him. (*VB*, p. 85)

Now we understand, at least from this description, that Tarwater is uncomfortable, disturbed. But we will misread the passage if we attribute his anxiety to his impending meeting with Rayber. The jump to be made is from his experience of the stars to his desire to confess his deed to Rayber and be congratulated by him. Why does his awareness of the stars motivate this desire? And why does he believe that Rayber will congratulate him? We have already seen that fire — in this case the fire of the heavens, the stars — usually signifies God's presence. (The devil uses fire, too, of course — he gets Tarwater to burn Powderhead down — but O'Connor almost always tips us off to the devil's fire by describing its color as pink or violet.) Tarwater no longer feels smothered by the heavens, but the beacons of God are trained on him like so many rifles. Through the stars God sits in judgment of Tarwater, and so, in his alienation from the Almighty, he feels lonely and desires to be comforted by his uncle, someone, he knows, who is alienated from God too. Even before their meeting the two are essentially in league, and that is why Tarwater expects that Rayber will approve of his broken faith with God's servant, old Tarwater.

The use of such correlatives has several advantages, among them compression and speed. When we see Tarwater on those front steps, the very way in which O'Connor places him there tells us what he's feeling. Also, the interior life of a multifaceted character may be fascinating in its twists and turns, but how can one write at length about someone like Tarwater as Henry James writes about Isabel Archer? It's not that Tarwater is a simple man in contrast to this complex woman; he's complex in his own way. But he's not articulate — we wouldn't expect that his ruminations come to mind in a form that would be interesting. (Of course, O'Connor uses Tarwater's dialogue with the devil to offset part of this handicap — the drama of the dialectic can engage us because we can appreciate the art with which the devil turns Tarwater's head even as we deplore it.) O'Connor replaces that kind of investigation of a soul with essentially poetic descriptions of the world from Tarwater's point of view. Thus she avoids having to cheat, to lend thoughts to a character that we know are the author's — as, say, John Updike does in his early novel *Rabbit, Run*. This use of description makes it possible for a host of characters to function as chief protagonists — characters who would otherwise draw small parts (as in Dickens) if they drew any parts at all.

In talking about "poetic description" we do not mean merely to ascribe the virtue of beauty to the writing; we might more accurately call it metaphoric description or — even better for the distance it supplies — figurative description. After all, language is in its essence metaphoric. Each word merges two identities: the thing itself — a chair, let's say — and the sound or configuration of letters — the word *chair* — that signifies the thing-in-itself. Metaphor takes this process one step further, equating two different things-in-themselves: the *flesh* is *grass*. Often in poetry the second term will be implied rather than stated. (Symbolist poetry turned this common practice into a moral imperative, dogma.) Thus Yeats in "The Old Men Admiring Themselves in the Water" can speak of old men as gnarled trees on a stream bank, equating the deterioration of the trees with human mortality. He is interested in gnarled old trees not only for their values as symbols. He is interested in the trees *themselves* precisely because the equation he's making between their forms and man's experience seems to be at work; they are an example of — they *embody* — the same reality, which is shared by and larger than both. We can therefore know our fate through theirs; we can see it in their figures. Accurate observation then becomes paramount, for if we want knowledge in this way, then the greater attention we pay these trees, the more we will be able to "figure out" our destiny. With Yeats — and entailed in many discussions of modern and contemporary writers — there is a great deal of talk about how metaphor enables the poet to reconcile contraries or to forge an alliance between opposites, make them interpenetrate — for example, the meaning of a man's life and the end of that meaning in death. What usually happens is that the apparent dissimilarity of the opposites succumbs to the metaphoric process, its ability — its inherent drive — to equate, to find similarities between, two different terms. For the basic assumption of any poet using metaphor is that the terms share something absolutely fundamental (and some writers like Robbe-Grillet have eschewed metaphor for this very reason). In most cases that something is the physical universe; both man and the trees are part of the natural world.

This brings us back to O'Connor. She assumed a logically prior truth, that a supernatural God had created the natural order. She was therefore able to attempt a poetic feat that makes the reconciliations of Yeats — or those of the other poet who is most praised for this, Wallace Stevens — appear of minor significance: the reconciliation of the supernatural and the natural. The work of Yeats, magnificent though it certainly is, finally suffers from the separation of nature and grace that occurred in the Enlightenment. Despite his investigations of the occult, his poetry is very much sealed within the natural; if this were not the case, his occult speculations would be more of an embarrassment to the modern sensibility than they already are. With the gods utterly dead, Stevens gamely fought his way out of the confines of his own skull, out of subjectivity into objectivity, out of the phenomenal into the noumenal, only to fall back once again into the eternal (not temporary) void of the self. O'Connor believed, as Saint Paul writes, that the things invisible are known by the visible, the supernatural by the natural, the Creator by the creation (see Rom. 1:20). For her nature bears the weight of glory; the

missing term in her use of metaphor is always God.

In O'Connor's figurative description, then, we ought to be on the lookout for transfiguration, the light of that glory glowing in its figures. One scene in the novel is an icon of just this. One morning Rayber is to take Bishop and Tarwater to visit the museum of natural history. On the way they stop for a while in a park near the museum. A "kind of island" (*VB*, p. 163), a memory of the pastoral within the urban, the park reminds both Rayber and Tarwater of Powderhead. Their experiences of it are reported — Tarwater's in a flashback — from each one's point of view. This memorial recollection of Powderhead becomes transubstantial as Tarwater's experience of the park continues; the spirit that makes Powderhead itself inhabits this space, too. Tarwater feels "a hush in his blood and a stillness in the atmosphere as if the air were being purged for the approach of revelation" (*VB*, p. 163).

Bishop then spots a fountain where water falls from the mouth of a marble lion, and he gallops toward it.

> The child stood grinning in the pool, lifting his feet slowly up and down as if he liked the feel of the wet seeping into his shoes. The sun, which had been tacking from cloud to cloud, emerged above the fountain. A blinding brightness fell on the lion's tangled marble head and gilded the stream of water rushing from his mouth. Then the light, falling more gently, rested like a hand on the child's white head. His face might have been a mirror where the sun had stopped to watch its reflection. (*VB*, p. 164)

The structure of the imagery, its iconography—the attention that O'Connor pays the sun, the uses of fire that come before it, and perhaps the memory of the Spirit's coming to rest on Christ in the form of a dove at his baptism—makes us wonder if O'Connor *intends* this celestial blessing on Bishop. O'Connor is trusting something here that the surrealists and other honest secular writers of this century have so distrusted: the satisfaction the mind takes in design. Any kind of pattern or form in art puts us on the alert to receive the designer's intention, his meaning, just as patterns in experience make us suspect the author of the beginning and the end. The context tells us that O'Connor does intend for us to know that God's favor rests on Bishop. As Bishop's face becomes a mirror image of the sun, so the figure of Bishop shows forth the glory of God the Son. O'Connor's method throughout the story is apparent in this scene in a condensed way. O'Connor is trusting that our good suspicion of mystery will lead us to recollect the alliance of circumstances and the pattern of imagery in the novel as a whole, as we can much more easily in this park scene, and finally cause us to see to what or to whom these figures testify.

The poetic radicals and thus the book's action come to fruition through what we might call prophetic fulfillment. This involves the growth of the images into the forms of the final scenes and, again, the way that O'Connor presses metaphor toward the literal. Each poetic radical will carry us through to the final vision of the book. Some do this in a more complicated way: they are drawn into relation with another image and qualified by it, occa-sionally swallowed by another, until yet another image unseams the carrier image and releases the original. In this way the country, the "grey country," works as an image of heaven. It is paired with the look in Bishop's eyes, hidden for a while in that image, and then both water and silence release it for its final consummation in Tarwater's concluding vision. For the purposes of this inquiry, however, I think it best to investigate in detail the action of hunger, because it will take us more easily into the heart of the book.

Hunger works as a metaphor that leads to a metamorphosis. It is an image for a state of being that over time comes to be an abiding and then a motivating force in the narrative, a dynamo of the novel's action. (Thirst, hunger's complement, works in this way as well.) Hunger also bears in on the basic problem of the novel: the reason for Tarwater's resistance to his prophetic calling, which, despite its importance, receives very little direct attention in the narrative.

The early scenes tend to deflect our attention from this issue. They show that while Tarwater definitely feels a sense of rivalry with his great-uncle, he loves the old man and finds the flamboyant aspects of prophecy highly attractive. But if we pay heed in the early passages to what Tarwater doesn't like about being called to be a prophet, we will see that the ending is manifestly prepared for at the beginning, and that hunger is O'Connor's principal means of expressing this basic problem of the book. Old Tarwater teaches that Jesus is the bread of life; when he dies, he says, he will "hasten to the banks of the Lake of Galilee to eat the loaves and fishes that the Lord had multiplied" (*VB,*

p. 21). Tarwater finds this reward for serving God disappointing in the extreme: "Had the bush flamed for Moses, the sun stood still for Joshua, the lions turned aside before Daniel only to prophesy the bread of life? Jesus?" (*VB*, p. 21). When his great-uncle exclaims that he has been "born into bondage and baptized into freedom . . . into the death of the Lord Jesus Christ," Tarwater feels a "slow warm rising resentment that this freedom had to be connected with Jesus and that Jesus had to be the Lord" (*VB*, pp. 20-21).

His refusal to acknowledge the sovereignty of Christ, to recognize that his freedom lies in obedience to Him, is the central problem of the narrative and accounts for his initial lack of a spiritual appetite. "In the darkest, most private part of his soul, hanging upsidedown like a sleeping bat, was the certain, undeniable knowledge that he was not hungry for the bread of life" (*VB*, p. 21). He realizes, however, that his great-uncle's prediction that he will become a prophet must entail acquiring this hunger: "What he was secretly afraid of was that it [the hunger] might be passed down, might be hidden in the blood and strike some day in him and then he would be torn by hunger like the old man, the bottom split out of his stomach so that nothing would heal or fill it but the bread of life" (*VB*, p. 21). Thus, for him to be hungry will be for him to desire the will of God, to accept his calling as a prophet.

At the exact moment that Tarwater meets Bishop and receives his calling, O'Connor connects the issue of sovereignty with being fed:

He only knew, with a certainty sunk in despair, that he was expected to baptize the child

he saw and begin the life his great-uncle had prepared him for. He knew that he was called to be a prophet and that the ways of his prophecy would not be remarkable. His black pupils, glassy and still, reflected depth on depth his own stricken image of himself, trudging into the distance in the bleeding stinking mad shadow of Jesus, until at last he received his reward, a broken fish, a multiplied loaf. (*VB*, p. 91)

Later Tarwater remembers this moment and how he had feared being lost to his own inclinations forever, yet it is only through being lost to those desires that he can be the man, the prophet, that God has created him to be (see *VB*, p. 221). As the bread of life will be his reward — a metaphor for what O'Connor, in reference to Pope Pius XII, also called the "super-aliveness of holiness" — so hunger for that bread will be a principal sign of his need to lose his life in order to find it. (As the passage on p. 162 shows, the devil is adamant that he not accept hunger as a sign.) For Tarwater is bound up in this paradox of human freedom: we can rejoice in the natural only by accepting its supernatural origins; we can be ourselves only by being the creatures God ordained us to be; we will find food satisfying, an agent of life, only if we take it as the Body of the way, the truth, and the life. Otherwise the natural can only provide carrion comfort; bread can be only a temporary means of delaying our death and so, at last, the ultimate sign of that death.

Tarwater tries to find food in Rayber's negation of belief. But like the breakfast cereal that Rayber dispenses, "shavings out of a cardboard box" (*VB*, p. 161), Rayber's agnosticism leaves Tarwater unsatisfied. He can't even take it seriously until he has drifted far enough away from the teachings of old Tarwater to look to Rayber with "something starved" in his eyes (*VB*, p. 115). Still, the sight of a loaf of bread in a bakery's window stops him in his tracks.

These pangs gradually become more and more frequent until Tarwater is constantly hungry:

> Since the breakfast he had finished sitting in the presence of his uncle's corpse, he had not been satisfied by food, and his hunger had become like an insistent silent force inside him, a silence inside akin to the silence outside, as if the grand trap left him barely an inch to move in, barely an inch in which to keep himself inviolate. (*VB*, p. 162)

This "silent force" works through the fiction in a way analogous to its operation in Tarwater. For readers it is something of a mystery, and therefore adds almost a suspense-story element to the novel's action: we want to see if and how this problem is going to be solved. In terms of commentary, O'Connor is silent — apart from the image system she employs — about the problem's cause and solution, as heaven turns out to be silent, the very land of that silence, in defending its claims on Tarwater. We should note in passing that the devil is constantly answering charges that are never advanced by God, although sometimes Tarwater refers the devil to old Tarwater's admonitions. Once again God is the missing term, the presence the reader must infer. He is present within this forceful silence and this mysterious hunger.

Tarwater's hunger grows relentlessly. He tries to stuff himself with food in order to get rid of it, but he vomits whatever he eats, after which his *emptiness* "reestablish[es] its rightful tenure" (*VB*, p. 174). His need to fill his emptiness finally becomes greater than the force of his own willfulness. In the end he goes back to Powderhead, back to the promontory with its forked tree, below which lie the cornfield, the outbuildings, and the burned house. Here the devil again speaks to Tarwater, urging him to go down and take possession of the land for himself — and for the devil, who promises never to leave him again. But just before this temptation, when Tarwater caught his first glimpse of the clearing and the burned house, "his dry lips parted. They seemed to be forced open by a hunger too great to be contained inside him" (*VB*, p. 237).

From the very first appearance of the devil, Tarwater has known that the ultimate choice in life is between Jesus and Satan, although the devil tries to convince him that he must choose between Jesus and his own desires. O'Connor never questions Tarwater's power to choose between heaven and hell; the novel would have no meaning apart from the reality of this choice. Yet the story also suggests that the devil speaks to desires inherent in Tarwater while the Lord simply makes implacable demands of him. We might almost be convinced that in the end God forces Tarwater to return to him. Here we have the freedom-of-the-will debate between Erasmus and Luther (and countless other theologians) — but we have it presented in a form that allows us access to this paradox without tending to dissipate its tensions. Again, Tarwater's hunger may be the best lens on the novel's vision in this regard. He is hungry in the most natural way: he wants and then desperately needs to eat. But the activity of eating carries within it the curse of the Fall and the hope of our restoration to another Eden — Paradise — through redemption. Like Tarwater, we cannot permanently satisfy our hunger; we have to repeat the activity of eating endlessly. And yet the enjoyment in eating points to a state of satisfaction of which eating is but a foretaste. Tarwater's final vision expresses this mystery: "The boy too leaned forward, aware at last of the object of his hunger, aware that it was the same as the old man's and that nothing on earth would fill him. His hunger was so great that he could have eaten all the loaves and fishes after they were multiplied" (*VB*, p. 241).

Thus the most common activity in the world — eating — ends up being the most available sign of our one final yearning: beatitude. That's why O'Connor could call *The Violent Bear It Away* "a very minor hymn to the Eucharist" (*Letters*, p. 387). For what we see in Tarwater's hunger is the most natural of desires completed by its supernatural extension of meaning. I would argue that the desire for God is as natural as the desire for food, and that the temptation to mistake this sign of beatitude for beatitude itself — which is idolatry, the worship of Satan — is as ever-present as gluttony. God's demands and the devil's temptations are both present within Tarwater from the beginning of the narrative. From the start he's both attracted and repelled by the notion of becoming a prophet. These contrary desires are simply extended through the rest of the

narrative. God actively waits for Tarwater's need of him to win out, while the devil encourages Tarwater's evil impulses, knowing that sin is taking Tarwater ever further from God. We are more familiar with the devil's tactics and our own fallen nature, of course, and that's why Tarwater's desire to be his own god may strike us as more human.

Even given this, God's action in Tarwater's life may still strike us as peremptory, cold. In one sense the battle for Tarwater's soul, which accounts for the violence in *The Violent Bear It Away* — the same violence as Satan's rebellion against God, man's complicity in that rebellion, and the violent recapture of man's soul through Christ's most violent death — this battle is never a fair fight. God has created Tarwater to be a prophet, set him in this world of fire and loss to baptize Bishop, and if he will not be a prophet, he can only become nothing. The devil has only illusion to offer, a flash of light across a lake between the last moment of day and the first of night (see *VB*, p. 156). Reality, in other words, is all on God's side. But as O'Connor once remarked, the church has never encouraged the notion that hell is not a going business. Rayber, who is the book's counterexample, chooses nothing again and again. His ascetic unbelief assumes the forms of not looking at any one thing for very long lest its inscape reveal its nature, and not feeling anything like love for very long lest he start loving the whole world as he loves Bishop. He does this because he wants nothing more than not to be. After Bishop's drowning, Rayber finally gets what he wants: he has cut himself off from all truly human modes of feeling for so long that the shock of hell comes when he realizes that he will not be able to feel remorse for the loss of Bishop. He has helped kill his last link with the divine and thus with the fully human. He has chosen this null state so often that God has finally let him have it. The tragedy of Rayber is as real as the tragicomedy of Tarwater.

The universe that we see in the microcosm of this image of hunger is also to be found in the macrocosm of the novel's total design. The achievement we have glimpsed in little is magnified exponentially when we realize that the same light that burns in each of these images or stars is to be found in the constellation they make together, the chart of human history in the celestial figure of Christ. I can do no more than resketch the outlines of that figure, but that will be enough, I think, for the full weight of O'Connor's success to begin registering.

Tarwater's call to be a prophet should not set him apart in our minds from the spiritual history of every man. In fact, he ought to be taken for a representative figure, another Adam. When he fears acquiring his great-uncle's calling, he tries, like Rayber, not to look at anything for long:

> It was as if he were afraid that if he let his eye rest for an instant longer than was needed to place something—a spade, a hoe, the mule's hind quarters before his plow, the red furrow under him—that the thing would suddenly stand before him, strange and terrifying, demanding that he name it and name it justly and be judged for the name he gave it. He did all he could to avoid this threatened intimacy of creation. (*VB*, pp. 21-22)

Adam, of course, was originally charged with this task. O'Connor seems to be saying that

prophecy is in its essence a recovery of man's proper role in creation—his completing creation by naming it for God, his giving God glory by praising him for it. (O'Connor was delighted to find that Saint Thomas ascribes the power of prophecy to the imagination [*Letters*, p. 367].) The prophet appears to have a grand part in the kingdom of God, but in fact he only has a part that shows more clearly than others the primary task for which every man was made.

Tarwater is thus not a peculiar figure but a representative one. Like the first Adam, he breaks the unique sanction of his covenant with his spiritual father: just as Adam ate of the tree of the knowledge of good and evil, Tarwater fails to bury his great-uncle. As a consequence his Eden, Powderhead, ceases to be a type of paradise and becomes instead an accusation of his spiritual nakedness from which he must escape—pursued by his uncle's silvery eyes from the midst of the fire's whirlwind. O'Connor uses this contrast of the pastoral setting with the city most explicitly in the transfiguration scene in the park, which is inhabited by the spirit of Powderhead, a spirit of revelation and mystery, of heaven. Several times she touches upon the representative status of Powderhead as a paradise lost. When Rayber visits the farm with Bishop, the child's eyes, a focus of heaven, reflect "the ravaged scene across the field," and "a dreaded sense of *loss* [comes] over him" (*VB*, p. 186; italics mine). When he lets Bishop be drowned by Tarwater, Rayber also lies waiting for judgment, "for all the world to be turned into a burnt spot between two chimneys" (*VB*, p. 200). And when Tarwater finally goes back to Powderhead, he looks across to the house from that same vantage point of the forked tree and sees "the sign of a broken covenant. The place was forsaken [lost] and his own" (*VB*, p. 237).

Tarwater has lost the bond with his great-uncle that the covenant was meant to supply, just as we have lost our original bond with God. That's why any place that we take for ourselves, as Adam claimed Eden for himself through the false assertion of his sovereignty, will be equally deserted, forsaken, by the spirit of God. For our task is to name those places and in the naming render them back to God. From the vantage point of the forked tree, Tarwater can see all that his disobedience has caused him to forfeit; from the vantage point of that "red-gold tree of fire," which "ascended as if it would consume the darkness in one tremendous burst of flame" (*VB*, p. 242) — from the Cross — mankind's loss becomes clear. At the forked tree Tarwater renounces evil, casting the "violet shadow" into the fire he quickly lights (*VB*, p. 237). He casts the devil into hell. Then he returns to Powderhead, where he learns that mercy and grace have been granted to him: a black neighbor, Buford, buried his great-uncle while Tarwater was drunk, and has been tending the cornfield in his absence.

After Buford moves off, Tarwater is finally given his ultimate sign of the bread of life that will be his reward someday: a vision of the faithful, including his great-uncle, sitting down to that meal. And thus he is restored to carrying out the mission for which he was made. He is to warn the children of God of the terrible speed of mercy. It comes so quickly be-cause God cannot help treating us with love — the love that lets Rayber have his own choice, and the love that grants the same to Tarwater.

In "Some Aspects of the Grotesque in Southern Fiction," O'Connor herself prophesied that the direction of many contemporary novelists, the best ones, would "be more toward poetry than toward the traditional novel" (*M & M*, p. 50). She was speaking, again, as much for herself as anyone else, and she did her part to fulfill the prophecy. *The Violent Bear It Away* surely ranks as one of the finest art novels of the twentieth century. It's a worthy successor to the novels of Joseph Conrad, the writer who most influenced her. Its concentric circles of meaning, the pools of Bishop's eyes, restore the circle as a sign of infinity's coherence — the same image that Conrad used in *The Secret Agent*, drawn over and over by a retarded man-child, Stevie, to express life's randomness.

The Violent Bear It Away was given a mixed reception. Many critics found it impossible to have sympathy for a character like Tarwater, which exempted readers — most particularly themselves — from taking to heart this hymn to the Eucharist. As the secular world became anxious about O'Connor, the church finally began to claim the novelist as her own. O'Connor received a "nasty paragraph" from *The New Yorker*, but she garnered generally favorable reviews (with some notable exceptions) and thoughtful criticism from the Catholic press and Christians in the academic world (*Letters*, pp. 385, 388). No doubt the role of the devil helped clarify for everybody whose side she was on.

Sister Loretta (above), Mary Ann's nurse, and Father Paul (below), a Trappist monk and a good friend of O'Connor's. O'Connor and her mother used to visit Father Paul (at the Monastery of the Holy Spirit in Conyers, Georgia) and have lunch with him and his superiors. The nuns of Sister Loretta's order also brought Mary Ann to the monastery —a visit Father Paul remembers vividly.

Editor and Exegete

IN 1960, the year that *The Violent Bear It Away* was published, Flannery received a proposal from a nun, Sister Evangelist, the Sister Superior of Our Lady of Perpetual Help Free Cancer Home in Atlanta. She asked if O'Connor would compose the story of a saintly little girl, Mary Ann Long. The sister explained that the child had come to the home in 1949 at the age of three, suffering from cancer. She had regained her strength for several years and had lived with the sisters until her death at age twelve. Mary Ann had been born with a tumor on one side of her face, and surgery to remove the eye above the growth had compounded her disfigurement. She was nevertheless a delight to know, full of love, not bitterness, and favored with an uncanny, spontaneous charm. O'Connor suggested that the sisters write the book themselves, volunteering her help only as an editor. To her surprise, Sister Evangelist accepted the challenge. After the manuscript had been completed, O'Connor sent it on with reservations to Robert Giroux, whose firm shocked her by agreeing to publish the book. O'Connor wrote an introduction for it, and it was published in 1961 under the title *A Memoir of Mary Ann*.

Although by no means a work of art, *A Memoir of Mary Ann* does its job: it convinces us of the little girl's sanctity while showing that Christ can use even the evil of unmerited suffering as a vehicle of grace. No doubt the editorial efforts of O'Connor and Giroux contributed to its improbable success. Still, both O'Connor's response to Sister Evangelist's proposal and her reflection on that response found in the book's introduction betray her anxiety about the book's reception. Toward the end of her introduction O'Connor alludes to Bishop Hyland's funeral sermon for Mary Ann, in which he acknowledged that the world would ask why Mary Ann should die. "He could not have been thinking of that world," O'Connor remarks, "much farther removed yet everywhere, which would not ask why Mary Ann should die, but why she should be born in the first place" (*M & M*, p. 226). Throughout the introduction, in fact, O'Connor addresses the prejudices of those who make up this other world, the intelligentsia. Her anxiety arose in anticipation of how the book might affect their opinion of her.

The tone of the book itself is tender in an unapologetic way. Re-reading O'Connor's introduction after reading the book gives us a helpful shock; we are doused by the icy, ironical waters of the contemporary idiom. We are listening to O'Connor be her sardonic self. "Stories of pious children tend to be false," she begins (*M & M*, p. 213). If the introduction were a review of the book, this wouldn't be a promising sentence (unless the writer was addicted, as O'Connor was, to ironic reversals). The introduction continues in this vein for some time. The first paragraph lets us know that O'Connor considers most such stories wrong in fact, or so badly written as to be embarrassing. "For my part," O'Connor writes, "I have never cared to read about little boys who build altars and play they are priests, or about little girls who dress up as nuns, or about those pious Protestant children who lack this equipment but brighten the corners where they are" (*M & M*, p. 213). It's as if she's saying, I know, I know what you're thinking: are *we* supposed to pay attention to a piece of hagiography? And one depicting a child at that? What could be more mawkish! How in the world has O'Connor, the great contemporary writer, gotten herself involved in a project like this? To defuse the presumptions of these questions, O'Connor enlarges the joke. She tells us how Sister Evangelist wrote to her, suggesting that O'Connor might be the one to write Mary Ann's story. "Not me, I said to myself," she informs us. And when the sister went on to suggest that O'Connor might make the story into a novel, she wasn't thrilled: "A novel, I thought. Horrors" (*M & M*, p. 214). She also makes fun of the phrase in which the sister couched her invitation to visit: would O'Connor like to "imbibe the atmosphere" at the home? (The nuns, when we think about it, showed quite a bit of humility in letting O'Connor insult them for several pages at the beginning of *their* book.)

O'Connor gets out front right away and establishes that she possesses that sine qua non of the intelligentsia, sophistication. You can't believe I'm writing the introduction for such a book? she asks us. Not any more than I. Through such disparaging rhetoric she pre-

pares us for the tack she's about to take. If she can convince us that she could never be accused of what she is in fact doing — writing an introduction to a piece of hagiography — then she can pretend, for a while at least, to be doing something else. It is precisely at this point that the essay's structure fragments. By the time the collage-like segments form a coherent picture again, the introduction is over. O'Connor walks over the water of this exercise without getting her feet wet, and we are transported with her.

O'Connor informs us that the picture of Mary Ann that Sister Evangelist sent along reminded her of a story — "The Birthmark" by Nathaniel Hawthorne. When Alymer, the husband in the story, speaks of the birthmark on his wife's cheek for the first time, he calls it the "visible mark of earthly imperfection." In this he mistakes her flaw for her essence. She is right to conclude that he cannot love her but must in some sense hate her if she, in her essence, is only a sign of imperfection. O'Connor then recalls that in *Our Old Home* Hawthorne included an incident in which a fastidious gentleman took the opposite attitude toward a wretched-looking child. She excerpts the section in which the narrator reflects on the gentleman's picking up and holding the mute and sickly child as if he were the child's father. All of the gentleman's natural inclinations are said to run against this gesture, especially his "habit of observation from an insulated standpoint which is said (but I hope erroneously) to have the tendency of putting ice into the blood" (as quoted in *M & M*, pp. 217-18). O'Connor further recalls that this fastidious gentleman was indeed Hawthorne himself, and quotes relevant sections of his diary to prove it.

O'Connor tells us that Rose Hawthorne, the novelist's daughter, wrote that in this account of the Liverpool workhouse were the greatest words her father ever wrote. His example was partly what inspired her to begin her lifelong missionary work: she brought terminally ill cancer patients in off the streets to which they had been abandoned and cared for them until their death. Called Mother Alphonsa, the Mother Teresa of her day, Rose Hawthorne founded the Dominican Congregation, called then the Servants of Relief for Incurable Cancer — in whose house Mary Ann came to live.

O'Connor then excerpts the part of Rose Hawthorne's diary in which she recounts her dealings with Willie, a hellion who was the grandson of her first patient. O'Connor finds this account of an evil child more to her taste: "Bad children are harder to endure than good ones, but they are easier to read about" (*M & M*, p. 222). In fact, O'Connor suggests in passing that Willie was the prototype for Rufus Johnson in "The Lame Shall Enter First" (*M & M*, p. 225). Here O'Connor touches base again with her readers, but we are already getting the sense that we will soon move with her beyond our common prejudices.

O'Connor next recalls receiving the manuscript. With all its defects, she notes, it still managed to convey the mystery of Mary Ann. O'Connor then switches from talking about the objectionable aesthetics surrounding the case to the case itself. Her legerdemain goes almost unnoticed, partly because she accomplishes this shift so swiftly and partly because

she shades in the change with language that sounds familiar. She extends her secular readers an invitation, one that sounds like the implied invitation of most modern art. "The story was as unfinished as the child's face. Both seemed to have been left, like creation on the seventh day, to be finished by others" (*M & M*, p. 223). This was disingenuous; the only reader in this position was O'Connor herself. Here the person and the writer had to be joined, and in a way that was threatening. The little girl who had fended off people with sass, the woman who was shy, the author who had been both criticized without cause and praised without being understood — she was being asked to give her imprimatur to a story that would parade her own beliefs. She was the reader who was going to interpret this story for her usual audience, and while she might protect herself in the introduction by way of rhetorical sophistication, the act of writing the introduction was going to be a plain and unadorned endorsement of that part of Christianity that intellectuals usually agree politely not to mention: popular piety. What she made of the story was that "they [the nuns] had set down . . . what had happened and there was no way to get around it" (*M & M*, p. 225).

O'Connor then begins to explain *exactly* what we are to make of the story, leaving us no room to follow our own existentialist dictates. She tells us that Mary Ann and "the Sisters who had taught her had fashioned from her unfinished face the material of her death. The creative action of the Christian's life is to prepare his death in Christ" (*M & M*, p. 223). In going on to spell out the place of the Cross in theology, O'Connor performs a triple operation. She provides the secular man and the untutored Christian with the correct way to interpret the story. She also enters into the mystery of which she speaks, for the essay is a "good-bye to all that"—a renunciation, if need be, of sophistication, a death to literary fashion. Yet this passive action has an aggressive aspect as well. O'Connor considered herself the heir of Hawthorne. She liked to quote his statement that he wrote romances and thus made room for his kind of exaggerations, because she did the same thing. Hawthorne is a watershed; in him we see Christianity under the assault of rationalism. Here O'Connor claims him not only for herself but for the faith, showing that in the end he feared the right thing: the rationalistic ice in his blood. Thus he was saved from Alymer's fate, saved from the hatred of imperfection and for the action of charity in which his life—most especially through his daughter's efforts—participated.

In talking about Rose Hawthorne's Willie and alluding to her own, O'Connor acknowledges once again that she is part of her time, that she has the same nihilistic bent as her peers. But, like Hawthorne, she fears the conclusions to which that has carried most of us; she fears the right thing—God—more than men. And so she too is saved for that same charity, that obedience to Christ. She alludes to the contemporary works of fiction about death, many with "death" in their titles. Yes, she says, our mortality is central, but death can mean sterility and meaninglessness, as it does in so many of these works, or it can be the kind of pilgrimage to God that it was in Mary Ann's life. It is only when we have this attitude toward death, in fact, that we can love

life. This truth is evident in *Wise Blood*, where self-denial, asceticism, means life, and self-fulfillment means death. It is borne out by the sisters of Mother Alphonsa's order, and by Hawthorne's work. It is proved, O'Connor seems to hope, by her own work. And it is this attitude, this vein of wise blood flowing from Hawthorne through her, O'Connor strongly implies, that must finally redeem literature itself. It must free literature from the modernist trap of self-consciousness, its evaporation of content in favor of self-reflexive form and absurdity—the latter-day heir of rationalism—which often makes modern and contemporary works mere rhetoric in the worst sense and sounds the death knell for literature.

At this point O'Connor's aggressive intent gathers momentum. She is not the dupe of sentimental nuns but the true spokesman for the very Christian tradition that has inspired the best in Western literature. From this pedestal she delivers her final judgments. Our nihilistic sensibilities have borne us along to a condition far worse than anything seen in popular piety; in its place we have "popular pity." She recalls that many modern works use the suffering of children to discredit the goodness of God, thus doing away with him. Ivan Karamazov cannot believe because children suffer; Camus's hero cannot accept that Christ is God because of the massacre of the innocents. Because we then no longer believe God to be good, "we govern by tenderness. It is a tenderness which, long since cut off from the person of Christ, is wrapped in theory. When tenderness is detached from the source of tenderness, its logical outcome is terror. It ends in forced-labor camps and in the fumes of the gas chamber"

(*M & M*, p. 227). Like the Alymers of the world, mere tenderness would destroy the sources of good in its attempt to abolish imperfections.

The essay has descended from the aesthetic to the ontological: what, in any guise, is what. Yet by implication we can follow an ascension back into these climes. The humor, in both the medieval and the contemporary sense, of the modern world must be redeemed. We look in the face of evil and "find, as often as not, our own grinning reflections with which we do not argue"; thus "the modes of evil usually receive worthy expression" (*M & M*, p. 226). But now the task must be to "look into the face of good, [where] we are liable to see a face like Mary Ann's, full of promise" (*M & M*, p. 226). This face too is grotesque, but it is a face in which the good will be "under construction" (*M & M*, p. 226). O'Connor finally makes the essay her literary credo, clearing the house of literature in the process, and setting up herself and those who share her views as its rightful inhabitants. The essay does for readers of O'Connor what she believes the story of Mary Ann does for its reader: it illumines "the lines that join the most diverse lives and that hold us fast in Christ" (*M & M*, p. 228).

As mentioned earlier, O'Connor once reflected in a letter that she was much younger at heart as an adult than she had been as a child. She qualified the observation with "younger . . . or anyway, *less burdened*" (*Letters*, p. 137; italics mine). We see her shedding some of that burden in this essay, the weight of what intellectual fashion would have us mistake for dignity. The Cross is heavy; the Cross is light.

O'Connor with friend Brainard ("Lon") Cheney in 1959. He and his wife lived in Nashville, and O'Connor visited them when she came to the city to speak at Vanderbilt University. The speaking tours were challenging, physically and otherwise, but O'Connor found them very rewarding.

O'Connor in 1961, on the porch of the Cline house. She once joked in a letter to a friend, "As for me I don't read anything but the newspaper and the Bible. Everybody else did that it would be a better world."

A Habit of Being

EARLY on we spoke of an assessment of O'Connor's growth as a Christian being the inevitable corollary of judgments about her growth as an artist. In examining her introduction to *A Memoir of Mary Ann*, we have attempted to read the text of O'Connor's character between the lines of the essay. Although she probably would not have approved of this procedure, she would have been happy to have left this avenue as the only means of drawing conclusions about the unity of her life and work. Apparently she sought to accomplish a kind of vanishing act, to live a life that, like a third-person narrator, would not be seen anywhere but would be felt everywhere through her fiction. She tried to block the opposite operation of investigating her work through the details of her personal life. In her letters she stressed the uneventfulness of her life, fostering the notion that her life had little to do with her fiction and that her personal story was of no interest or relevance. "As for biographies," she wrote to a friend, "there won't be any biographies of me because, for only one reason, lives spent between the house and the chicken yard do not make exciting copy" (*Letters*, pp. 290-91). It is clear that O'Connor would have had her life read as a supreme example of the triumph of the imagination over individual circumstance.

It does stand as such in one way. And yet there is a native perception — the cause of books like this one — that supposes that a correlation must exist between the fascination of the work and the life out of which that work was created. While I believe this to be the case, we have to see the uselessness of this view to the writer himself. As I see it, O'Connor thought that her vanishing act was the essence of a successful life, of a life filled with charity. This sounds something like the mysticism common to our times, but Flannery's ideas were more fully grounded than that. When she wrote about charity to her close friend, who is simply identified as "A" in the letters, she pointed out that the charitable soul, the sanctified soul, does not become that way by self-abnegation, by reducing the self to a null quantity. (In another letter she pointed out that this is the real difference between Christianity and Eastern religions: the Christian faith stresses the fulfillment, not the obliteration, of the individual.) The command "Do unto others" presumes self-love, which the Bible takes as a given. Our popular psychology, which teaches the need for self-esteem, takes as its ultimate end what the Christian faith presupposes as a starting point. O'Connor argued that real charity moves us beyond preoccupations with the self and its suffering to the self-forgetfulness of serving others. Self-fulfillment cannot therefore be achieved directly by accomplishing the self's own ends: it will come only as a by-product of acting charitably, in which another's good directs our action. The ambitious anonymity of monks and nuns says something that is as true for the laity as for the religious.

O'Connor elsewhere likened the act of writing to the action of charity to explain the way in which the self becomes simultaneously lost in and taken up into the sacrificial character of love: she pointed out that she was never more truly herself than when she was writing, and yet she was never less self-conscious, because she was sacrificially directed toward — or, more simply, *serving* — the good of what she was making (as the doer of charity is concerned wholly with the good of its recipient). The conditions of art were analogous to the conditions of beatitude. Thus in a sense O'Connor believed that the less interesting she thought herself to be, the better she would be as a person and as a writer as well. In fact, self-preoccupation would have been a sure way for her to destroy her life and her vocation. So she, this most hermetic of writers, always scorned any talk about the "loneliness of the artist." Eliot addressed the same matter when he asserted that poetry should be impersonal, rising above the merely autobiographical and idiosyncratic toward the common experience of all, the universal.

But it is precisely the critical biography that must be conscious of matters about which the writer himself must avoid becoming self-conscious. That native correlation of the life and the work will hold true here. It has its place for us, as it could not have for O'Connor, because we can glimpse the fulfillment of O'Connor's personality in what were for her self-forgetful actions. In the end it would be untrue to her own theories if no relation existed between her life and her work, for in her life of self-denial (that life of passive diminishment) she did not give up "real life," but in becoming truly alive to the world through her work she in fact became most herself.

Sally Fitzgerald, O'Connor's chief biographer, called the volume of O'Connor's letters *The Habit of Being.* In her introduction to the book Fitzgerald notes that the title is her extension of the Thomistic idea of habits of mind or qualities of the intellect, an idea to which O'Connor referred constantly. Fitzgerald notes that O'Connor surely had the "habit" of art, the acquired quality of seeing ultimate reality in the narrative terms of her craft. The book's title grew out of her attributing another "habit" to O'Connor:

> Less deliberately perhaps, and only in the course of living in accordance with her formative beliefs, as she consciously and profoundly wished to do, she acquired as well, I think, a second distinguished habit, which I have called "the habit of being": an excellence not only of action but of interior disposition and activity that increasingly reflected the object, the being, which specified it, and was itself reflected in what she did and said. (*Letters,* p. xvii)

One might have capitalized "being" in this passage, because the Being that specified any such "habit" would have to be the object of those formative beliefs, God. This "habit of being" is a synonym for sanctity. Fitzgerald's paraphrase indicates, I think, a proper reluctance to judge someone's soul. But perhaps in these circumstances we can at least talk about the highly developed inner life that is unmistakable in O'Connor's letters and that matches, that *fits* with, the fiction. Outwardly quiet, even quietist, O'Connor's life had its intense and passionate side.

The crucible of that passion was discipline. O'Connor worked, when she was well enough to work, hours as regular as a banker's. The calamitous high jinks of mountainside car accidents, Bible salesmen absconding with wooden legs, and mummies being spirited out of museums, as well as the closely observed violence of a child's head being smashed against a stone — these came not out of wild nights of inspiration but from a daily routine, a daily *strict* routine, of a sober woman sitting down at her typewriter from shortly after breakfast until lunchtime. The famous *Paris Review* interviews with writers make clear that good writing gets accomplished in a multitude of ways. Still, as an editor of a collection of the interviews noted, there are two discernible classes of writers in terms of work habits: the gushers and the bleeders. Gushers spill out great quantities of work in short and often unpredictably episodic periods of time; bleeders coax out regular if small offerings. The principle of the tortoise and the hare seems to apply here: the gushers generally produce a small quantity of work, whereas the bleeders often produce a shelfful of books in the course of their working lives. O'Connor was most definitely a bleeder, and she recommended her course of action to others:

> I'm a full-time believer in writing habits, pedestrian as it all may sound. You may be able to do without them if you have genius but most of us only have talent and this is simply something that has to be assisted all the time by physical and mental habits or it dries up and blows away. . . . I write only about two hours every day because that's all the energy I have, but I don't let anything interfere with those two hours, at the same time and the same place. This doesn't mean I produce much out of the two hours. Sometimes I work for months and have to throw everything away, but I don't think any of that was time wasted. Something goes on that makes it easier when it does come well. And the fact is if you don't sit there every day, the day it would come well, you won't be sitting there. (*Letters,* p. 242)

As O'Connor indicates in this passage, the writing did not go well for long stretches of time, and this discouraged her. After completing *The Violent Bear It Away*, she wrote about experiencing "tides of revulsion" while composing the work (*Letters,* p. 368). She was dogged by worry as to whether the book had any life in it at all or could be made to come alive. Rayber and his part in the middle section of the novel were particularly difficult for her. Fundamentally, she was out of sympathy with Rayber's frame of mind — she didn't really know how such a person fitted himself into the world, and so she struggled to make him more than a stick figure. The short stories generally involved somewhat less frustration, and every so often she would give herself a "holiday" from the second novel by working on a story.

Her illness, of course, further slowed her halting rate of composition. No doubt this figured in the letter she wrote to fellow novelist Richard Stern upon hearing of yet another of his books coming out: "What are you fixing to do, publish another novel? Do you want to be known as One-a-year Stern? I am doing my best to create the impression that it takes 7 years to write a novel. The four-hour week. You are not helping the Brotherhood. Examine your conscience. Think. Meditate. Shilly-shally" (*Letters*, p. 532).

But for the most part O'Connor took the false starts, the constant revision, and the discarded work in stride because she knew these things were intrinsic to her manner of composition. She kept her planning of the fictions' development to a minimum. "I don't have my novel outlined and I have to write to discover what I am doing," she wrote to her agent, Elizabeth McKee. "Like the old lady, I don't know so well what I think until I see what I say; then I have to say it over again" (*Letters*, p. 5). Other statements make clear that she often did have something like an outline in mind, although her original conceptions of what characters would be like and what actions they would engage in were subject to any number of changes as she wrote. We can point to Rayber as a case in point. At first she conceived of him as a strict Echo of the devil's opinions. But when she constructed him as such, she found that the attraction of the idea of an Echo was greater than the actual use she could make of Rayber in this way; the good of the book called for him to be a more fully developed moral entity.

After she had surmounted the difficulties in a piece, she did indeed enjoy the results. "I certainly am glad you like the stories," she wrote to a friend, "because now I feel it's not bad that I like them so much. The truth is I like them better than anybody and I read them over and over and laugh and laugh, then get

embarrassed when I remember I was the one who wrote them" (*Letters*, p. 80). She made a similar admission to another friend, with this apology: "I feel this is not quite delicate of me but it may be balanced by the fact that I write a great deal that is not fit to read which I properly destroy" (*Letters*, p. 78). Her unequivocal enjoyment of some stories was no small sign of success, since subsequent readings of many pieces made her worry for years after they were published. Indeed, she often made changes in a story between its publication in a magazine and its appearance in a collection. ("Judgement Day," one of her last stories, is in fact a wholesale reworking of "The Geranium," the title story in her master's thesis.) Most good writers know all about the continual worry over a piece's failures—Auden remarked that poems are never completed, merely abandoned. The state of satisfaction that O'Connor arrived at with some of her stories is thus a thing to be wondered at and aimed for. Certainly it was also something earned.

When O'Connor finished her morning's work, she and her mother often drove into town to have lunch at a restaurant called the Sanford House. It was one of her few chances to get out, and the drive and the automobiles in which she and her mother made the trip afforded her many pleasures, especially after she took command of the wheel. This came late: she was thirty-three when she took her first driving test, an event marked by something of the rollicking disaster we find in her stories:

My latest accomplishment is that I flunked the driver's test last Wednesday. This was just to prove I ain't adjusted to the modern world.

I drove the patrolman around the block. He sat crouched in the corner, picking his teeth nervously while I went up a hill in the wrong gear, came down on the other side with the car out of control and stopped abruptly on somebody's lawn. He said, "I think you need sommo practice." (*Letters*, p. 289)

When she passed the test on her next try, her comic fascination with automobiles (she liked to watch stock-car races on television to see the drivers' faces) got a chance to manifest itself. Her comments about cars considered or purchased by Regina add touches of grinning, sardonic, and macabre humor to her letters. She says that Regina and she are looking for a black car because Regina "will not have one that looks like an Easter egg" (*Letters*, p. 291). She notes that a workman recommended his used car to the women by saying, "It's so pretty that when you're in it, it's just like being in a funeral parlor" (*Letters*, p. 293). And she expresses her satisfaction that the first car they buy together "is black, hearse-like, dignified, a rolling memento mori" (*Letters*, p. 294).

O'Connor devoted her afternoons to resting, reading, writing letters, and receiving visitors. *The Habit of Being* makes clear how important she considered the friends she made through correspondence and occasional visits. She underlined that abiding significance by passing along, in a letter, a prayer to the Archangel Raphael, whose traditional functions include guiding the individual to those he is supposed to meet in life: "O Raphael, lead us toward those we are waiting for, those who are waiting for us: Raphael, Angel of happy meeting, lead us by the hand toward those we are looking for. May all our movements be guided by your Light and transfigured with your joy" (*Letters*, p. 592). O'Connor claimed to have prayed this prayer every day for many years.

Taken together, the letters constitute O'Connor's lifelong effort to give of herself to her friends in the best way she knew how — writing. For the most part the letters have an offhand, colloquial tone; they are often filled with the burlesque of country talk. O'Connor's humor once again indicates something serious. Timid as she was, she used irony to short-circuit any rhetorical formalities and so break down barriers to intimacy. She sought to win through rhetoric a measure of what touch allows to lovers: a reaching toward self-revelation. What might seem the casual roughness of her comments is often suddenly interrupted by effuse apologies when she fears having offended. She was anguished by any hint from a correspondent of the world of meaning behind Eliot's lines "That is not what I meant at all. / That is not it, at all."

We see different facets of O'Connor in her responses to correspondents she related to in different capacities — as colleague, contemporary, teacher, and respected author. The most "public" letters, the ones in which she responded as a well-known writer, tell us almost nothing about her, except that wild interpretations of her stories drove her toward despair. When she responded as a teacher to students who wrote to her after hearing one of her public readings, she spoke very much to the person behind the intellectual questions. When young Alfred Corn (mentioned earlier) wrote to her about losing his faith as a result of his college studies, she imagined in her reply the possible circumstances that might have contributed to his newly adopted agnosticism. In the subsequent letters to Corn she managed to be a levelheaded and always personable apologist for the church, a teacher who could be herself and never for a moment stop teaching during office hours.

A certain tentativeness characterizes her letters to colleagues, other writers and intellectuals, with whom she corresponded — partly, one supposes, because she was always aware of how her views differed from theirs, and she did not want to open herself up to easy assaults. These letters are written from a protective crouch. Some are strategically polite in winking at her basic concerns. Examples are the cheery notes she wrote to Robert Lowell, despite the fact that his leaving the church always caused her pain. In letters to other colleagues she spoke more directly about herself, her work, and her feelings, although when she made any statement about her personal beliefs in this context, she made sure the arguments were as rigorous and inarguable as possible. Her letters to the novelist John Hawkes — those on the devil, for example — are the more valuable because, respecting his talent, O'Connor constructed them almost as tightly as anything in her formal essays. When she was openly at theoretical loggerheads with a colleague, she stopped short of insistence, but she could be blunt when the occasion absolutely demanded it. Her letter to John Lynch has the tone she used when her patience was exhausted:

> I write the way I do because and only because I am a Catholic. I feel that if I were not a Catholic, I would have no reason to write, no

reason to see, no reason ever to feel horrified or even to enjoy anything. I am a born Catholic, went to Catholic schools in my early years, and have never left or wanted to leave the Church. I have never had the sense that being a Catholic is a limit to the freedom of the writer, but just the reverse. (*Letters*, p. 114)

In the last years O'Connor achieved a greater ease in discussing her faith with colleagues, wondering aloud at the contradictions in their own thinking as much as rueing the embarrassments of the church. To Dr. T. R. Spivey, a professor of English at Georgia State University, she wrote, "They [modern people] are all so busy explaining away the virgin birth and such things, reducing everything to human proportions that in time they lose even the sense of the human itself, what they were aiming to reduce everything to" (*Letters*, p. 300). Likewise, she found the Beat writers untrue to any consistent religious vision:

> Certainly some revolt against our exaggerated materialism is long overdue. They [the Beat writers] seem to know a good many of the right things to run away from, but to lack any necessary discipline. They call themselves holy but holiness costs and so far as I can see they pay nothing. It's true that grace is the free gift of God but in order to put yourself in the way of being receptive to it you have to practice self-denial. (*Letters*, p. 336)

It is in O'Connor's letters to close personal friends that we come to know her best. Finer aspects emerge in correspondence to particular people; different kinds of friendships are nurtured and endure. In her correspondence with the playwright Maryat Lee, we see Flannery as a girlfriend: combative, gossipy, conspiring, delightfully malicious, and warm. A fellow Southerner, Maryat Lee lived in the North but had strong ties to Milledgeville: her brother was president of Georgia College. Something of a radical, she delighted in scandalizing the citizenry when she came to town for a visit. She once accepted a ride to the airport from a black man, and she appeared in various get-ups, including a great Russian fur hat. Flannery and Maryat differed on how much the civil-rights movement might accomplish through strictly political action, but in her first letter to Maryat, Flannery reported a local story that assured her new friend of their basic agreement on desegregation. The ironic treatment she gives the incident is characteristic of Flannery's letters to Maryat: not everything needed to be said between these two friends.

> Once about ten years ago while Dr. Wells was president [of Georgia College], there was an education meeting held here at which two Negro teachers or superintendents or something attended. The story goes that everything was as separate and equal as possible, even down to two Coca-Cola machines, white and colored; but that night a cross was burned on Dr. Wells' side lawn. And those times weren't as troubled as these. The people who burned the cross couldn't have gone past the fourth grade but, for the time, they were mighty interested in education. (*Letters*, p. 195)

As the correspondence developed, Flannery took delight in playing the redneck to Maryat's revolutionary. Maryat entered into the game as well, which gave birth to the run-

ning joke of Flannery's addressing Maryat by various corruptions of Rayber, such as Raybucket, Raybog, and Raybush. In turn, Flannery signed her own name with plays on Tarwater, like Tarbat and Waterbucket. The joke enters into the following passage, which is filled with a lighthearted raillery that bespeaks Flannery's love for her friend:

> Lord bless us, what next? Here I have been commiserating with my image of you that was so po and energyless it couldn't go to Washington to march for freedom with all its natural cousins and you all the time were fixing to hire yourself out as a super char to a super Catholic family. I can think of a lot of things I'd prefer your services at than housekeeping. No wonder she got another girl. You probably blended their garbage and baked it. The next book [Maryat Lee's] would have been *The Day We Were Poisoned by the Housekeeper*. (*Letters*, p. 538)

In Flannery's running correspondence with her once-closest friend, a woman identified only as "A" in the letters, we see the person who in an essential way would never be older than twelve. Whatever interfered with her closeness to "A" (except, at last, "A's" flight from the church), Flannery went out to do battle with. Ordinarily so self-protective, she wanted nothing to stand between them. Her own status, for which she had worked so hard, finally meant very little to her if it threatened to inhibit their friendship. Flannery put down her public image many times implicitly, once very explicitly: "If the fact that I am a 'celebrity' makes you feel silly, what dear girl do you think it makes me feel? It's a comic distinction shared with Roy Rogers's horse and Miss Watermelon of 1955" (*Letters*, p. 125). Having helped create their openness with one another, Flannery could say, "Know the terrific pleasure . . . that your presence in my existence gives me all the time" (*Letters*, p. 367). "A's" disaffection for the church apparently stunted the growth of the friendship, but not because Flannery made faith a condition. The two simply came to share less than they once did.

It's impossible in this space to do justice to the wealth of friendship exchanged in the letters. Sally Fitzgerald, Cecil Dawkins, Robie Macauley, William Sessions, and many others occupied enduring places in Flannery's affections. Unlike many famous people, she was as interested in their lives as her own.

Here we might stop to wonder what the lack of married love meant to Flannery. She protested against an accusation made by "A" that her fiction made little of erotic love by neglecting it; she replied that for her the erotic and all that it implies was the most holy of subjects, and she felt inadequate to deal with it — therefore her silence. Though she overcame her initial silence about physical suffering, Flannery never won through this most difficult of diminishments to its transfigured expression. Unless, that is, we believe that this type of sacrifice, whether made voluntarily or only accepted, as in Flannery's case, contributes to a lively apprehension of the City of God.

What then can we say of Flannery's inner life? No one can read the letters without being convinced that here was a woman who had, by her life's end, seen through her own foibles, pretensions, and flaws. She knew who she was.

Strong-willed and irascible, Flannery nevertheless cultivated a closemouthed spirit of penitence that gradually freed her of egocentricity, the burden of self. Ascribing a penitential spirit to Flannery may surprise many who have read the letters, because there is hardly anything in them of a "woe is me, O wretched man that I am" character. The letters are exuberant, not morbid. They manifest an outward directedness, a spirit of inquiry and fun that today we associate more with a natural youthfulness than with anything like penitence. But we should remember that we are dealing here with a person who was an "ancient" twelve-year-old, someone who in her childhood notebooks wished for nothing so much as to be left alone, to have other people mind their own "bidnis." Real self-knowledge brought home her need of others, and her struggles against the paralysis of her self-protective nature enabled her to become young (or direct) in her gestures of friendship. She gained the strength to reach out to others for love.

O'Connor also developed the strength to write according to her lights. Although she was hurt by bad reviews of her fiction, she carried on with her work with a singular sense of purpose, all the while having to bear with those who told her wherein she had failed in her "bidnis" and didn't know it. After *Wise Blood* she wondered briefly about the value of writing about "freaks" rather than "folks." As she matured, that doubt was replaced with an absolute conviction of the worth of what she was saying and the certainty that, for good or for ill, she *had* to say it in just this way. As Walker Percy notes in *Lost in the Cosmos*, few writers have coped with their vocation so well.

Her personal and professional growth contributed toward the greatest (and essentially religious) achievement of her life: her ability to live with tremendous affirmation the life her vocation and illness dictated. She demonstrated, if such a thing can be demonstrated, that one's "own life" as ideally conceived by the self is a pale thing compared with the life God offers.

Yeats said that a writer must choose between perfection of the life or the work. This was a false dichotomy for O'Connor. She believed that her duty was first to save her own soul; work mattered only in how it participated in this process. We have evidence in the letters that this perspective gradually allowed the various elements in O'Connor's life to assume their proper place. Her love for people gradually displaced the various means by which first the child and then the young woman sought to convince herself of her own self-sufficiency — those protests against her own needs that cried out those needs all the more. Even as she became more familiar with the difficult and complex vagaries of life, O'Connor seemed to exhibit an ever-greater degree of simplicity, evident in her direct requests to friends about her own needs, her abiding sense of the purpose in her work, and her apparent calm in the face of her declining health.

The passionate side of O'Connor's life was the passion of her long death to self. She found the grace to offer up a difficult nature, a maddening vocation, and the many passive diminishments her illness brought with it. In her own stubborn way, she followed Mauriac's advice to "purify the source."

The narrow, self-righteous religion of Mrs. Turpin was something O'Connor encountered in the South. She also encountered several incarnations of Mrs. Turpin, one of them during a stay in the hospital in 1964: "One of my nurses was a dead ringer for Mrs. Turpin. Her Claud was named Otis. She told me all the time about what a good nurse she was. Her favorite grammatical construction was 'it were.' She said she treated everybody alike whether it were a person with money or a black nigger. She told me all about the low life in Wilkinson County. I seldom know in any given circumstances whether the Lord is giving me a reward or a punishment. She didn't know she was funny and it was agony to laugh and I reckon she increased my pain about 100%."

"Revelation"

THE simplicity in Flannery O'Connor's life toward its end is matched and more by the purity of vision exhibited in her last stories, collected in *Everything That Rises Must Converge*. Widowed spouses and their contentious offspring are once again, as in *A Good Man Is Hard to Find*, the principal combatants. The settings of the stories are familiar, too — farms very like Andalusia and Rayber's generic Southern city. Yet we may hardly notice the virtuosity with which O'Connor varies the basic pattern of her short fiction because we keep moving deeper into the truth of this form. *A Good Man Is Hard to Find* is enriched by its sense of place; *Everything That Rises Must Converge* discovers to a greater degree the worth of those who inhabit this now-familiar landscape. The quick revelations of *A Good Man* give way to an intimacy with the characters that makes us live with and through them, that holds us within their limitations. Thus the breakdown of these very limits becomes, through the vicarious sympathy we are asked to extend them, affecting in the deepest sense. The almost cosmic distance we are allowed from Mrs. McIntyre and Mrs. Shortley in "The Displaced Person" vanishes. Of course, Hazel's lowering coffin-lid and Tarwater's dropping sky do enclose us within these characters, too, but only for claustrophobic moments. In the last collection the dimensions of the characters are roomy enough for us to identify with them, inhabit them, for stretches of time. With this new degree of intimacy comes compassion, that form of knowledge that does not allow us to judge without judging ourselves. Our verdicts open up the heavens once more for the advent of mercy. In taking on our humanity, Christ takes it with him into the presence of God; by virtue of this, the limitations, the shackles of these figures, are often seen at last to bind them to Christ.

"Revelation" is, in a way, a simple story. It's also a story that only a great artist in the full possession of her powers would have the audacity to write. It sums up the artist's entire practice in the way that four brush strokes can become an aged Japanese painter's masterpiece. Arranged on chairs and benches in a doctor's waiting room are several people from different strata of society. The only comment on the setting comes from the story's main character, Mrs. Turpin, who thinks that a wealthy doctor should provide his patients with a larger room, one that would more easily accommodate her tall and obese person. But a moment's reflection will disclose the setting's immediate associations. A doctor's waiting room is a kind of limbo in which we wait for judgments and treatments that either will send us back, restored, to life or will signal the end of life. The atmosphere that O'Connor evokes here may remind us of that of Sartre's *No Exit*: doom presides in both. But there is a way out of O'Connor's vestibule of eternity, and thus her use of this enclosure suggests more an earthly purgatory than Sartre's hell. That O'Connor must have spent an outsized portion of her life waiting for *the word* in such places gives this setting an added poignancy.

Mrs. Turpin has come with her husband, Claud, to have an ulcer on his leg treated. While there are several other people in the waiting room, three besides Mrs. Turpin are crucial to the action. These characters have a lineage, if you will, within the rest of O'Connor's work. A woman whom Mrs. Turpin considers white trash functions as a sounding board; her crude, interruptive responses in the developing conversation remind us of Mrs. Shortley in "The Displaced Person." Although she would seem a bit further down in the hierarchy of Southern society than the wife of a farm's foreman, she shares with this kind of woman a grandiose sense of her own dignity and a keen delight in subverting the pretensions of others. This character has had other predecessors as well: Mrs. Pritchard in "A Circle in the Fire," Mrs. Freeman in "Good Country People," and Mr. Greenleaf (the change in sex matters little to his use) in the story known by his last name. This slovenly woman sits with her unkempt little boy and the child's grandmother. The runny-nosed child inspires a derisive attitude in Mrs. Turpin, an echo of the relationship between owner figures and their help in other stories: even when they seem to get on like friends, they are separated by the differing fates of their children.

A "stylish woman" is the first to enter into conversation with Mrs. Turpin, appearing to be wholly in sympathy with her opinions, echoing her thoughts. Although the stylish lady turns out to have a hidden agenda, our initial identification of her with Mrs. Turpin is crucial. Together they play the role that belongs to the farm owner; they can be thought of as a composite character. Mrs. Turpin and Claud do in fact own a farm; they have "a little of everything . . . a couple of acres of cotton and a few hogs and chickens and just enough whiteface [cattle] that Claud can look after them himself" (*CS*, p. 493). Thus they are almost but not quite typical: they lack the usual complement of white help. The "white-trash woman," as I've indicated, plays this part. But the stylish woman's appearance — she is wearing red-and-grey suede shoes that match her dress — also tends to raise the status of our composite character a notch. The stylish woman also holds to the maddening conventional wisdom that characterizes several women in the second collection of stories.

As O'Connor kept writing, this fund, this bundle of truisms, began to receive more and more sympathetic treatment. True, Mrs. Cope in "A Circle in the Fire" and Mrs. May in "Greenleaf" are finally undone by what looks like their pragmatic efficiency. But the mother figures who are more typical of this collection — those who appear in "Everything That Rises Must Converge," "The Comforts of Home," and "The Enduring Chill" — prove to be far more human than their offspring, and they are generally let off, we might say, with a lighter sentence. (Indeed, the later stories tend to play more against the illusions of young people. Anyone trying to reduce O'Connor's stories to sublimated acts of hostility against her mother — which is a temptation — has to reckon with her more-than-stern treatment of young, albeit failed, artists and intellectuals.) The stylish woman's humanness is all the more evident because she is the mother of the last important character, an ill-tempered girl of eighteen or nineteen.

The girl — ironically named Mary Grace — is another of O'Connor's unhappy young intellectuals. She is fat, with a face "blue with acne" (*CS*, p. 490); she has just finished her first year at Wellesley. In the waiting room she tries to get on with her furious reading of a book entitled *Human Development* while Mrs. Turpin and her mother blather away. In our recording of lineages she descends from the smart twelve-year-olds in "A Temple of the Holy Ghost" and "A Circle in the Fire." This figure takes a nasty turn in "Good Country People" with Hulga, who has cast aside her given name, Joy, and decided on a fate as ugly as her chosen name. Thomas in "The Comforts of Home," Julian in "Everything That Rises Must Converge," and Asbury in "The Enduring Chill" are the fat girl's predecessors, too, but undoubtedly her next of kin is Rufus Johnson in "The Lame Shall Enter First." Rufus knows the truth but spurns it; he's a deliberate sinner, a juvenile delinquent who shows up Sheppard, the man who adopts him, for a false messiah. Mary Grace delivers a similar revelation when she slashes through the three-handed conversation in the waiting room by hurling her copy of *Human Development* at Mrs. Turpin, scoring a bull's-eye. We are left to conclude, however, that her redemption is much farther off than Rufus Johnson's, en-

tailing as it does the long detour found in books like *Human Development*. (The title of the book is one more act of revenge of this most rueful of social-science graduates.)

The story's theme is that found in "The Displaced Person" and nearly every other O'Connor story: that meanness that characterizes the relationships of the author's owners and their help, of her mothers and their children, of all her combative pairs. This meanness originates in the desire to better a rival and drives the characters to degrade their opposition in an attempt to gain the never-to-be-reached point at which they can feel superior; it is a meanness that originates in the guilty secret of the self's imperfection and manifests itself in all the illusions of divinity to which pride resorts. Original sin, pride, is the theme of this story and of so many others. Of course we think of Tarwater too in this connection, of his refusal, for a time, to accept that Jesus must be the Lord. But we should think even more of these combative pairs. O'Connor is hailed as a writer who gives us access to lives very far removed from our own, those of backwoods prophets. Nevertheless, the preponderance of her stories have a thoroughly *bourgeois* character. In fact, we might talk about many of the conflicts in the stories as examples of class struggle if the same paradigm of conflict did not also manifest itself between the members of a family and between others who are, in a sociological sense, equals. Class struggle, the Freudian model and its Oedipal complex, and plain enmity — all are seen anagogically as the ways in which original sin manifests itself.

The great achievement of "Revelation" is that O'Connor manages to maintain our interest in a central problem that is blatant. The skill of the rendering keeps us reading although we know from the first pages, especially if we have some acquaintance with her other work, what's at issue. Indeed, O'Connor may count on our knowing and jumping to the conclusion that "Revelation" will have a violent end much after the fashion of "The Displaced Person." Violence will arrive—we are right—but here it will not be the end.

Mrs. Turpin likes to daydream about her social rank. She wonders what fate she would have chosen if God had asked her, before her soul entered the world, to pick between life as a black woman or life as white trash. This racism, which permeates the hearts of the characters in this story, is nearly asphyxiating, and yet it is not as powerful an evil as that which motivates disgust. Mrs. Turpin would choose to be herself but black—largely, we suspect, because she has taken an aversion to the white-trash woman, whom she considers "worse than niggers any day" (*CS*, p. 490). We are also privileged to know that Mrs. Turpin, instead of counting sheep at night, makes a habit of contemplating the social rankings in their proper order, building up through and beyond the people like herself who own property. The ambiguities of once-moneyed people whose fortunes have fallen and of the blacks who are more wealthy than she cause her such discomfort that she's willing at that point in her thoughts to bundle everyone into boxcars and haul them off to a gas oven. We may tend to discount this sudden glimpse into the evil in the woman's heart, but O'Connor is plainly saying that gas ovens are just logical extensions of common selfishness, the truth behind that disgust and our modern tenderness.

Then the game of one-upsmanship begins. It starts with Mrs. Turpin's assessment of the white-trash woman. Later, when she thinks about the fact that Jesus had not made her "a nigger or white-trash or ugly" (*CS*, p. 497), her heart is filled with what she mistakes for gratitude. Indeed, Jesus himself spoke of her condition in the parable of the Pharisee and the publican praying in the temple. Like the Pharisee, Mrs. Turpin is filled with a self-satisfaction that vitiates her small virtues. Her love for her husband and her steadfast adherence to duty are swallowed up—the snake taking its mouse-sized prey—by a consuming vanity. O'Connor might have taken Mauriac's title, *A Woman of the Pharisees*, for this story.

The satisfied air of the initial pleasantries exchanged by Mrs. Turpin and the stylish lady communicates itself to the white-trash woman. When Mrs. Turpin describes her farm, this woman quickly interjects her opinion of pigs: " 'One thang I don't want,' the white trash woman said, wiping her mouth with the back of her hand. 'Hogs. Nasty stinking things, a-gruntin and a-rootin all over the place' " (*CS*, p. 493). Mrs. Turpin explains that Claud and she have a pig parlor in which their hogs' feet never touch the ground, and that Claud hoses them down every afternoon. Her hogs are cleaner than the white-trash woman's child, she thinks to herself. Mrs. Turpin further remarks to the stylish woman that she and Claud have only a little cotton planted, and that's a great bother because she has to be cordial to the blacks who come to harvest it. The white-trash woman instantly seizes this opportunity to slip the knife in again. "Two thangs I ain't going to do: love no niggers or scoot down no hog with no hose" (*CS*, p. 494). Mrs. Turpin's complaints about her help are, we know, her way of bragging. Her hidden intentions foiled, Mrs. Turpin nevertheless seems to find a way — although the tension among the three increases markedly — to counter the remark. The stylish woman and Mrs. Turpin exchange a look that indicates that "they both understood that you had to *have* certain things before you could *know* certain things" (*CS*, p. 494). But the white-trash woman has been more successful than we may at first believe. The disgusting habits of hogs, akin as they are in Mrs. Turpin's mind to the uncleanliness of white trash, to the uncleanliness that she no doubt takes for the opposite of godliness, add greatly to the weight of the coming revelation. She is relieved that Jesus has not made her to be unclean white trash or a member of a persecuted race or an ugly person, but in the end she will have to experience a degradation greater than these.

As I've noted, on a first reading the stylish woman appears to merely echo Mrs. Turpin's opinions. But we will miss what nearly amounts to a subplot of the story if we do not, on a further reading, see that the stylish woman is always addressing her daughter through her comments to Mrs. Turpin. The story's moment of havoc — the assault on Mrs. Turpin — leads us to suspect that the fat girl may be at the doctor's office because of emotional problems (the doctor is awfully quick with the needle when she becomes violent). So it's significant that the first real opinion her mother offers refers indirectly to personality disorders. "I don't think it makes a bit of difference what size you are," she says to Mrs. Turpin. "You just can't beat a good disposition" (*CS*, p. 490). Like Mrs. Hopewell in "Good Country People" and Mrs. Fox in "The Enduring Chill," the stylish woman thinks her daughter's problems stem from her being an intellectual. She mistakes one of her daughter's characteristics — being smart — for the ground of her personality. Since she doesn't approve of that basis because it seems to cause unhappiness, she traps her daughter into believing that there is something fundamentally wrong with her.

The daughter seems to be ensnared by this illogic. In rebellion she seizes upon being an intellectual and insists upon being identified as such, thereby making the same mistake as her mother: interpolating a causal relationship between her intelligence and her unhappiness where none exists. Thus she cannot understand the real sense in which her mother is wrong. The young woman simply assigns a positive value to what her mother devalues. She cannot maintain this posture very easily, however, as her actions show; her mother's judgments are the basis of her own, and therefore her different evaluation of herself must seem capricious. Living what seems to the subconscious a lie entails great pain. And of course every suggestion by her mother meant to free her from her condition only makes that condition worse, since it underlines the negative value of what they both mistake for her real self. The daughter, with this last and fearful twist of neurosis, *is* an intellectual, so she's smart enough to be attuned to every sign of her mother's disapproval, to see in some sense that her mother is wrong, and to despise the pharisaical people about her. She has everything but true self-knowledge, which makes her condition that much worse. We are asked to infer something like this because she begins making exaggerated, ugly faces at Mrs. Turpin at just those points at which the woman's limitations claw into her sensibilities (as well as our own).

Mrs. Turpin intuits correctly that the girl knows her in a way that her own bad faith will not permit her to know herself. The girl's first evil look makes Mrs. Turpin think that the girl "had known and disliked her all her life — all of Mrs. Turpin's life, it seemed too, not just all the girl's life" (*CS*, p. 495). The vicious pettiness of the interminable, three-handed conversation continues to grate upon the girl (and us). In its course her mother delivers an unqualified indictment of her daughter: she is "the worst thing in the world," an "ungrateful person" (*CS*, p. 499). Mrs. Turpin, completely unaware of the effect the conversation is having on the girl — she never suspects for a moment that her pleasantries carry something else along with them — follows up on this indictment by trumpeting her own virtues, her utterly different disposition, and her extreme gratitude. "I just feel like shouting, 'Thank you, Jesus,'" she cries, "'for making everything the way it is!'" (*CS*, p. 499). She cannot admit that the status quo is fallen, for she would be the queen of the status quo. After all of this we want to hurl *Human Development* at Mrs. Turpin and fly upon her and choke her, just as the girl does at this instant. The book might have been more justly aimed at the girl's mother, but the misdirection makes little difference

considering the character of the alliance between Mrs. Turpin and the stylish woman.

If O'Connor had been less of an artist, perhaps even if she had written this story earlier in her career, the piece could well have ended with this judgment. Or it could have ended just afterward, when Mrs. Turpin has the courage to ask the girl, "What you got to say to me?" (*CS*, p. 500). That's the moment of grace, the moment when the Spirit in the form of a water stain that resembles a fierce bird descends on Asbury in "The Enduring Chill." It's the moment when the grandmother in "A Good Man Is Hard to Find" reaches out to the mass murderer, the Misfit, just before he kills her. (This characteristic moment of grace is always surprising, but inevitable.) But here Mrs. Turpin isn't gunned down, not literally at least. The girl instructs her, "Go back to hell where you came from, you old wart hog" (*CS*, p. 500).

After the girl delivers this verdict, this *word*, we are, with Mrs. Turpin, as with Tarwater, allowed to ascend out of this purgatory, granted a vision of mercy. In an odd way it's much more natural to make this journey with Tarwater; he's not like us, and so it's less difficult to believe that strange and wondrous things can happen to this backwoods prophet. But Mrs. Turpin is like us: middle-class, middlebrow. We may see her depravity much more easily than our own, but then the girl proves how easy it is to judge others correctly and misread oneself. Who can deny that he, even if in a more hidden way, usually acts out of self-interest? Self-sacrifice would be less central if we all didn't have an understanding in our bowels, as the psalmist says, of how rare it is. For this reason, perhaps, O'Connor treats Hazel Motes and Tarwater and Rufus Johnson more kindly. She is hardest on the bourgeois, which is to say that she's hardest on people like herself.

After returning home and trying in vain to rest, Mrs. Turpin goes out to the pig parlor to give the Lord a good piece of her mind. While she stands washing down the hogs, she receives a vision. It is a vision of the procession of humanity marching on its way up to glory, with the bourgeois, the people who, "like herself and Claud, had always had a little of everything and the God-given wit to use it right," bringing up the rear (*CS*, p. 508). Mrs. Ruby Turpin truly loves her Claud, and she has been a good steward of the wealth that God has given her, but as she watches the procession, she sees that even the small virtues of people like herself must be burned away (are burned away in that great morning), because finally even the best things about us must become all gift, all grace, pure as God's refining fire. Standing in the pig parlor, Mrs. Turpin receives first the knowledge of the justice of the girl's sentence, but this revelation of her depravity leads to an ascending vision. The vision reverses her own sense of social rank: first come the white trash, next blacks, then freaks and lunatics "shouting and clapping and leaping like frogs" (*CS*, p. 508), and at the tail end the bourgeois. This is the pattern of loss and gain that structures Mrs. Turpin's experience in the story. The first shall be last, and the last shall be first. Mrs. Turpin finds that she has to *know* certain things, the self-congratulatory il-lusions by which we hide our own failings from ourselves, before she can *have* certain things — namely, heaven.

The language in which this final vision is rendered should remind us of "A Temple of the Holy Ghost" and its "line in the sky like a red clay road hanging over the trees" (*CS*, p. 248). Here, too, there was "a purple streak in the sky, cutting through a field of crimson and leading, like an extension of the highway, into the descending dusk.... She saw the streak as a vast swinging bridge extending upward from the earth through a field of living fire. Upon it a vast horde of souls were rumbling toward heaven" (*CS*, p. 508). From this connection we can infer that O'Connor has traveled a great way along this road since first sighting it; she has reached the point at which her vision of the blessed has grown encompassing enough to include the bourgeois, people like herself. It seems that O'Connor has at last succeeded in expressing her own condition; she has finally glimpsed in the grotesque face of good something akin to her own likeness. This sassy little girl, this socially awkward adolescent, this prophet freak finally seems to have believed that she had indeed taken that narrow road, struggling with her crutches and her "poverty of means" toward that still point of light, toward that country where "the silence is never broken except to shout the truth" (*VB*, p. 242).

*   *   *

While Flannery was working on the last stories for *Everything That Rises Must Converge* in the late fall and early winter of 1963, she began to feel weak again. Apart from the continuing troubles she had with both hipbones, for a lupus patient she had been in reasonably good health for some years, especially after the introduction of Merticorten. But now her health was declining. The doctors found that her hemoglobin count was low and eventually traced the problem to a fibroid tumor. Though benign, the tumor had to be removed; the doctors couldn't elevate Flannery's hemoglobin level otherwise. This was a risky procedure. A patient's immune system obviously plays a key role in healing the wounds of surgery; to trigger it into action would incur the hazard of reactivating Flannery's lupus. Nevertheless, Flannery entered the Baldwin County Hospital on February 25, 1964. She insisted that the procedure be performed at her local hospital rather than at Piedmont Hospital in Atlanta, because Regina was then nursing her sister, Miss Mary Cline, as well as Flannery.

What had been feared came about: Flannery had just recovered nicely from the surgery, it seemed, when her adversary struck again. The lupus attacked her kidneys, hindering their capacity to filter the poisons that are introduced into the blood by proteins. Flannery did finally go up to Atlanta for a month spanning May and June, and then came back home. She felt that the attack was not as severe as the first onslaught in 1951. But she had to know that she was far from being the strong young woman she had been at that time, and therefore that her life was in danger. When a priest brought her communion in July, she asked for extreme unction.

Reading the letters she wrote during these last months does not fully prepare us for her death. She maintains her sense of humor; her concerns are for her correspondents. True, there are hints that she saw the end coming. In a P.S. in a letter to her friend Louise Abbot she did go so far as to request prayers, saying, "I am sick of being sick" (*Letters*, p. 581). Still, her death breaks the letters off seemingly in midcourse. The last is a note to Maryat Lee, who at that time was being harassed by telephone. Flannery's voice is as strong as ever: "Cowards can be just as vicious as those who declare themselves — more so. Dont take any romantic attitude toward that call" (*Letters*, p. 596). Soon after writing these lines she lapsed into a coma and was taken back to Baldwin County Hospital, where she died of kidney failure on August 3, 1964. She was thirty-nine.

A Legacy of Grace

*E*VERYTHING *That Rises Must Converge* was published in 1965, the year after O'Connor's death. It met with praise from all quarters. O'Connor would have hooted at the cliché that great artists are rarely appreciated during their lifetimes. She might have pointed to Michelangelo and Shakespeare and Hawthorne and James, who, if they did not always get exactly what they wanted, were nevertheless recognized as the preeminent artists of their day. O'Connor thought of herself as a success, and indeed, in her lifetime she gained a devoted readership, won recognition by some of our best critics, and was awarded grants, fellowships, literary prizes, and honorary doctorates. Since her death, however, her stock has risen still higher, so much so that we might say that only now is the true nature of her genius coming into view. During the years since 1970 — no doubt partly due to the publication of *Mystery & Manners* in 1970, *The Complete Stories* in 1971, and *The Habit of Being: Letters of Flannery O'Connor* in 1979 — she has been read even more widely and with greater appreciation. A growing body of criticism now addresses her life and work. Her essays, for which we have Robert and Sally Fitzgerald to thank, and her letters — another invaluable resource provided by Sally Fitzgerald — have deepened many readers' understanding of her work. Her fictions, insane on the surface but

reaching down to the depths of truth, are repaying this attention.

O'Connor worked within the major literary current of her time in prose narrative: naturalism as it has come down through Flaubert, Chekhov, Conrad, and Joyce. Her stories have the epiphanic structure of Chekhov and Joyce, her novels the imagery systems of Flaubert and Conrad. This is a rich inheritance, and most authors in our time have done well to position themselves as its legatees. For O'Connor, however, the will and testament of these literary patriarchs was fraught with difficulties. With metaphysics dismissed, she found that the form was at a stage of hermeneutic crisis; morality had collapsed into personal choice, and that had led to man's freedom being considered nonexistent or an absurd irrelevance in a universe from which the gods had long departed. This in turn vitiated the underlying assumptions of the form: there is little point in telling a story if a character cannot make meaningful choices. The best one can do is bewail this state of affairs with Beckett.

But a literature of despair must at last dissolve the basic assumption of naturalism: that the author and reader share a common world — a nearly synonymous reality — and thus that conventions of physical description, character development, and dramatic action mimic the ways in which both author and reader perceive

O'Connor in 1962 or 1963, one or two years before her death. She wears the hat (decorated with peacock feathers) she has on in the portrait painted by friend Robert Hood.

O'Connor died on August 3, 1964. A fitting epitaph is found in a letter she wrote a few years earlier: "Let me tell you this: faith comes and goes. It rises and falls like the tides of an invisible ocean. If it is presumptuous to think that faith will stay with you forever, it is just as presumptuous to think that unbelief will."

this reality. Only if there is such common agreement can naturalism's presentation of reality bring the delights of recognition and identification: in sum, a vicarious encounter with an experienced meaning, which presumably will nourish the soul of the reader and may aid his will in its future choices. Having excluded the mythic dimensions of Christianity as its context — for example, the assumption that personal choices have infinite consequences, a value through all eternity — naturalism had begun to disintegrate. Without a supernatural cause and explanation, the bond of author and reader was breaking down, because attempts to define nature apart from the supernatural failed. Author and reader no longer shared the common medium of physical experience; the realities in which they dwelt were unique to each and thus hopelessly plural for the purposes of art.

The conventions of naturalism themselves, the honest unbelieving writer had to admit, should have been replaced long ago. (Secular writers have been working at this for a good century.) Yet, even if the underlying assumptions of naturalism were nonsensical, authors could depend on their audience's being familiar with the conventions of naturalism by which their naive predecessors had told stories that looked and felt "real." And so we have seen authors dally with these conventions in order to investigate their own consciousnesses or simply to play the game, to construct funhouses. Most of the gamesmen have had the good grace to inform the reader that there was no such thing as "nature" or "reality," at least not one common to the reader and themselves, and have been at pains to distance the reader from their stories at those points at which he might be most inclined to take them seriously. Self-reflexive forms are essentially apologetic, a kind of protestation that the author cannot, after all, be expected to render up truth. O'Connor was certainly aware of this:

> Many modern novelists have been more concerned with the processes of consciousness than with the objective world outside the mind. In twentieth-century fiction it increasingly happens that a meaningless, absurd world impinges upon the sacred consciousness of author or character; author and character seldom now go out to explore and penetrate a world in which the sacred is reflected. (*M & M*, p. 158)

O'Connor not only recognized this but also felt obligated to be responsible to it and, I would argue, to redeem it. The Christian artist in a pagan or neopagan society is always in a difficult position. He must always answer Tertullian's question "What has Jerusalem to do with Athens?" by saying, Everything. The tradition he inherits insofar as it expresses a true appreciation of the creation will be adaptable for his purposes. O'Connor was very much a "creationist" in precisely this sense: the heavens declare the glory of God to everyone. But the Christian artist will be obliged to pick and choose useful elements in the pagan tradition, not adapt it wholesale, for the devil is an angel of light, and thus beauty is not always truth, nor all we need to know about it. In *Wise Blood* O'Connor began to point to the country, a reality, *both* within and around us, that we share. She grabbed hold of sin as the last smelling salt that might arouse our dormant sense

of the holy. In *A Good Man Is Hard to Find* she then examined what our souls crave — a habitation in this world — and showed the kingdom of darkness, of sin, as a cheap substitute that alienates us from what we desire. In the last collection of stories, *Everything That Rises Must Converge*, O'Connor showed us this same source of deprivation, this privation of being — sin — but also revealed something more of the fullness of being to which mercy would bring us. She did the same thing in *The Violent Bear It Away*, teaching that the one story of mankind will also necessarily be present in the multitudes of our own stories; we are all offered those endlessly multiplied loaves and fishes.

While secular literature neared exhaustion, O'Connor reestablished links between the natural and the supernatural, and thereby showed us a way to save the form of naturalism and its endless exfoliations by preserving its traditional notion of content. More, in *The Violent Bear It Away* she created through the art novel a fictional world unlike anything in modern and contemporary fiction. In this world the supernatural and the natural interpenetrate; the characters cross and recross the barriers between the two until each is clearly immanent in the other. Fantasy literature has often tried to recapture this sense of the supernatural's presence in and completion of the natural, but in our time it has usually been marred by a cartoonish texture that is a sad testimony to the very disjunction between nature and grace that fantasy literature protests against. I would argue that Eliot and O'Connor are the only ones in our time who have given us the seamless Christian worlds that we find in medieval romances like *Sir Gawain and the*

Green Knight, and O'Connor does it through stretches of narrative, which may be a greater achievement than Eliot's poetic moments of the same. In *Sir Gawain* we have the feeling that the journey of the knight from the castle to the chapel perilous, from the ordinary to the fantastic, involves nothing more than a hard ride — no through-the-looking-glass hocus-pocus. *The Violent Bear It Away* has this same continuity of the temporal and the eternal: we can take the interstate to get to Powderhead. And notice that the terms of this comparison land us right where modernism, despite its arduous strivings, failed to take us: to the resurrection of the epic. For medieval romances are epics, although it's true they are secondary ones, deriving from the epic of the gospel. For a Christian, chasing after Homer is not a possibility; we who believe must leave that to Pound and Charles Olson and his kind. They haven't yet succeeded at what they have attempted — if, in fact, they're still trying; O'Connor did.

The best thing about the way O'Connor took is that it is not, like so much in modernism, self-exhaustive. We can learn from her fiction, be inspired by it, and practice our art in confidence that that loaf will never cease to multiply. Near the end of her life O'Connor saw that she would have to move on to a further stage of development. "I appreciate and need your prayers," she wrote. "I've been writing eighteen years and I've reached the point where I can't do again what I know I can do well, and the larger things that I need to do now, I doubt my capacity for doing" (*Letters,* p. 518). We who follow her must take up this challenge, further restoring the sense of the holy to contemporary sensibilities. We must work at reconstructing that grotesque face of good that O'Connor calls us to finish. Neither the *nouveau roman* nor the nonfiction novel nor magical realism nor the next passing wave of secular literary fashion will resurrect literature out of the tomb of this century. Only through the contributions of an incarnational art, practiced by the grace given in the Incarnation, shall literature, like all things human, rise and converge with its end.

Images

When we talk about the writer's country we are liable to forget that no matter what particular country it is, it is inside as well as outside him. Art requires a delicate adjustment of the outer and inner worlds in such a way that, without changing their nature, they can be seen through each other. To know oneself is to know one's region.

Mystery & Manners

If you're a writer and the South is what you know, then it's what you'll write about. . . . It's perhaps good and necessary to get away from it physically for a while, but this is by no means to escape it.

Letters

The artist himself always has to remember that what he is re-arranging *is* nature, and that he has to know it and be able to describe it accurately in order to have the authority to rearrange it at all.

Mystery & Manners

The novelist is required to create the illusion of a whole world with believable people in it, and the chief difference between the novelist who is an orthodox Christian and the novelist who is merely a naturalist is that the Christian novelist lives in a larger universe. He believes that the natural world contains the supernatural. And this doesn't mean that his obligation to portray the natural is less; it means it is greater.

Mystery & Manners

Fiction is supposed to represent life, and the fiction writer has to use as many aspects of life as are necessary to make his total picture convincing. The fiction writer doesn't state, he shows, renders.

Letters

When fiction is made according to its nature, it should reinforce our sense of the supernatural by grounding it in concrete, observable reality.

Mystery & Manners

The Catholic novelist in the South is forced to follow the spirit into strange places and to recognize it in many forms not totally congenial to him. He may feel that the kind of religion that has influenced Southern life has run hand in hand with extreme individualism for so long that there is nothing left of it that he can recognize, but when he penetrates to the human aspiration beneath it, he sees not only what has been lost to the life he observes, but more, the terrible loss to us in the Church of human faith and passion. I think he will feel a good deal more kinship with backwoods prophets and shouting fundamentalists than he will with those politer elements for whom the supernatural is an embarrassment and for whom religion has become a department of sociology or culture or personality development. His interest and sympathy may very well go — as I know my own does — directly to those aspects of Southern life where the religious feeling is most intense and where its outward forms are farthest from the Catholic, and most revealing of a need that only the Church can fill.

Mystery & Manners

I can't allow any of my characters . . . to stop in some halfway position. This doubtless comes of a Catholic education and a Catholic sense of history — everything works toward its true end or away from it, everything is ultimately saved or lost.

Mystery & Manners

He only saw the river, shimmering reddish yellow, and bounded into it with his shoes and his coat on and took a gulp. He swallowed some and spit the rest out and then he stood there in water up to his chest and looked around him. The sky was a clear pale blue, all in one piece—except for the hole the sun made—and fringed around the bottom with treetops. His coat floated to the surface and surrounded him like a strange gay lily pad and he stood grinning in the sun. He intended not to fool with preachers any more but to Baptize himself and to keep on going this time until he found the Kingdom of Christ in the river. He didn't mean to waste any more time. He put his head under the water at once and pushed forward.

"The River"